Praise for *Live Your Gift*, Dana V. Adams, and Life Mapping

"I'm a big believer in mapping out your goals, milestones, and accountability metrics to maximize your gifts and achieve your life's purpose. This is the process that transformed the life of Dana V. Adams; maybe it can do the same for yours."

—Darren Hardy, *New York Times* bestselling author of *The Compound Effect* and founding publisher and former editor of *SUCCESS* magazine

"If you want to finally unlock growth and live with a possibility mindset, read *Live Your Gift*! Dana V. Adams will show you how she conquered her hidden fears to start living the life she desired. With warm intelligence and refreshing clarity, she'll inspire you and teach you how to do it, too."

—Dr. Srini Pillay, Harvard psychiatrist, executive coach and CEO of NeuroBusiness Group, brain researcher, and author of *Tinker Dabble Doodle Try* and *Life Unlocked: 7 Revolutionary Lessons to Overcome Fear*

"In *Live Your Gift*, Dana V. Adams brings to life a holistic tool that takes you from belief to action, and has the potential to aid you in transforming your life. In it, she borrows the famed quote from Marianne Williamson's book *A Return to Love* when she states, 'Our deepest fear is not that we are inadequate. Our deepest fear is that we are powerful beyond measure.' Ah, yes, how true. Unfortunately, too many of us go to the grave with unsung songs, unfulfilled dreams, and unopened inner gifts. *Live Your Gift* provides a key that helps us to unlock and release this 'power that is beyond measure' and empowers you to live your gift AND your dreams!"

—Debrena Jackson Gandy, national bestselling author of *Sacred Pampering Principles* and *All the Joy You Can Stand*

"Dana practices what she preaches in her book *Live Your Gift*. She is a perfect example of what life mapping can do for your life."

—Jessica Butts, CEO of Front Seat Life and author of *Live Your Life from the Front Seat* and *Don't Do Stuff You Suck At*

"As a person in recovery from alcoholism, Dana's book reached me on a profound level. Here is a book with practical steps on how to live a better, joyous life. *Live Your Gift* provided a doable life plan along with the courage and grace to follow it. I plan on sharing *Live Your Gift* with my sober community, as well as friends who may not have addiction issues but need a straightforward, thoughtful book like Dana's to lead them to a happier, more fulfilling life."

—Roberta Romero, (former KING 5 NBC-Seattle) reporter, sober since January 2, 2004

"If you've got questions about how to fulfill the life you were meant to live, Dana V. Adams's *Live Your Gift* will seem heaven-sent. It is packed with the kind of explicit guidance and practical applications you can immediately use to discover who you really are."

—Carol Adrienne, author of *The Purpose of Your Life* and co-author of *The Celestine Prophecy: An Experiential Guide*

"Dana V. Adams learned the power of life mapping first as a student and then as a teacher. She inspires, empowers, and leads a new generation to discover their gifts in her book *Live Your Gift*. With the right teacher and tools, everyone can live the unique gifts graciously given them by God. *Live Your Gift* is destined to be a bestseller. I encourage you to read this book and share it with family, friends, and colleagues."

—Bill Cohen, Author of *Life Mapping*

"Dana is an inspiration, champion, and spokesperson for those most vulnerable. Through her own personal journey and in support of those without voices, she continues to support and drive forward the importance of self-worth and value. There are endless applications for the important lessons Dana shares in *Live Your Gift*. Her insights not only inspire but also give readers the tools to thrive, regardless of the season of life one may be navigating. Her book is especially enriching for those facing any barriers to living as their healthiest, best selves, and serves as a useful, hands-on guide for achieving new levels of well-being."

—Laurene Burton, executive director—governance and community affairs, EvergreenHealth

"Six years ago, Dana introduced the life mapping process to a handful of brokers in my office. Our brokers now travel to a resort to fully invest in the curriculum and study. Dana's organization and presentation of the life mapping concepts have been very well received and embraced by our broker staff. Practical application of the concepts has resonated in the lives and businesses of those who attended, evidenced by their personal life maps and vision boards. It is a study of growth and achievement in all parts of life that is very personal and unique to the student. I highly encourage your attention to Dana's work."

—Michael Connolly, designated broker, Windermere Real Estate, Kirkland, WA

"Throughout my life mapping experience with Dana, I realized that the phrase 'you don't know what you don't know' could not ring more true. Taking time to gain the insight into what my life could look like—the way I want to design it—was one of the most inspirational experiences I've had. With Dana's guidance, I was reminded of the things I can do every single day to help me be a better person and draw pure joy into my daily life. I was also reminded that not only does keeping your dreams at the forefront of your mind keep you motivated and inspired, but also—eventually, with some persistence and hard work—they really do come to light. I am so thankful for the work that Dana does, and I highly recommend the process to anybody who's ready to get back on track to living a life they love."

—Darren Kentner, real estate industry professional

"I think that life mapping is a valuable tool to make a commitment in getting things done in your life, whether it be for business, family, or personal goals of any nature. I enjoyed going through the motion of making my lists for what I want to achieve in my life. For me personally, the sessions have solidified what I have always done in my life. You can't have success with your goals if you don't lay out a plan for achieving them. Life mapping has certainly taken that to the next level."

—BJ Connolly, co-owner, Windermere Real Estate, Kirkland, WA

"I thoroughly appreciate Dana's insights, pacing of materials, and direction in our business planning and life mapping. Structured work time, samples of life mapping, and anecdotes from her own life are great, too!"

—Kristi MacPherson, Realtor®

"Life mapping is always evolving. Time spent reflecting on my beliefs gave me insight into what's true for me. Now I know I have a North Star."

—Jan Carroll, real estate broker

"Life mapping is a constant process. It's like learning music or a foreign language or studying for school: you must 'use it or lose it.' Just because we stuff ourselves silly at our family's Thanksgiving dinner doesn't mean we don't need to eat until next year. Life mapping is the same; you can't devour the rich content at the workshop and expect to go home and have lasting impact unless you continue to feed yourself the material and practice the concepts."

—Diane Charouhas, senior real estate specialist

"Just the little bit I have witnessed is inspiring. Having seen what a big part of the author's life the book has become makes it easy to see how her passion for it has taken her on what looks like an amazing journey. I do believe in it and the power it has for people that follow through with it. I think in my practice of trying to do it each year it is a good reminder of what is important to me. I do have my vision board looking back at me right now as I type this and see it as my desktop on my computer each time it is turned on. Dana V. Adams definitely brought value to me."

—David Pope, Realtor®

"Thank you, Dana, for taking us beyond the book and guiding us through the steps of life mapping. I walked away from this year's intensive retreat focused and empowered. I would describe life mapping as starting with discovering the *why* to establish one's goals and then implementing a number of manageable tasks to achieve them. By starting with the why, the goals are centered around what is meaningful. The work is, therefore, purposeful because the intention behind it is authentic."

—Jennifer Burton, branch manager, Penrith Home Loans

Therese –

Made me think of you when I read this! Cheers to the journey & glad you're part of mine! :)

Lis

live your gift

live your gift

Discovering Your Authentic Life Through Life Mapping

DANA V. ADAMS

Foreword by Bill Cohen, Author of *Life Mapping*

live your gift

Published by Life Mapping Institute, LLC.

Attention Corporations, Universities, Colleges, Schools, Addiction Treatment Facilities, and Professional Organizations: Quantity discounts are available on bulk purchases of this book for educational or gift purposes or as bonuses and giveaways for increasing membership. For more information please contact us:

www.lifemappinginstitute.com
support@lifemappinginstitute.com

Cover design by NewBreed.Design
Editing by J. M. Emmert
Interior Design and Composition by Accelerate Media Partners, LLC

ISBN: 978-1-7329947-6-8

SEL027000 SELF-HELP / Personal Growth / Success

Printed in the United States of America

Dedication

To my four incredible boys—James, Trent, Gage, and Michael—who inspire me every day to be the best mom I can be. You motivate me to learn from yesterday, imagine a better tomorrow, and enjoy every moment we have today. **I love you!**

Contents

Foreword

I have been living the *Life Mapping* process for over thirty-five years, and it has proven to be invaluable. The peace and freedom generated by the process helps us create not only an enjoyable life but also one that is abundant. I have seen the process help people under the poverty line experience the fulfillment of their dreams. Nothing is as powerful as witnessing people transform their lives into the ones they have longed for.

This world is in desperate need of a tool to help the disenfranchised find the path to fulfillment. The proof of this can be seen by the failures so easily observed in our society: the number of people addicted to drugs; the number of people who bully others, physically or mentally; the number of people who commit mass murder; the number of people currently taken by human traffickers. If we want to see change, it needs to start with each of us individually. People living their own life maps will be part of the solution for the many problems our society currently faces.

Several months ago, I received a Facebook message from Dana V. Adams asking if I was the Bill Cohen who wrote *Life Mapping*. That message was the beginning of a friendship which is destined to last a lifetime.

Dana began by telling me the story that led to her creating her first life map. While browsing a bookstore, she noticed an interesting little yellow book titled *Life Mapping*. She immediately had to have a copy and devoured it in short order. She followed the process outlined in the book to develop her first of many life maps. She has lived the life mapping process for almost two decades, and it has helped her achieve her life goals. But she has moved beyond just living *Life Mapping*; she has also been teaching it. Her Life Mapping Institute Workshops help others create their own life maps. Dana shared the joy she receives from seeing others benefit from the creation of their own life maps. When we are doing the work we are gifted to do, it changes us. We escape the self-doubt that keeps us from truly reaching fulfillment in this life. We discover our gifts and begin sharing them with others, and Dana's teaching of the life mapping process in her workshops has done just that. Dana has learned she is a gifted teacher, and the proof is in the number of people who keep coming back.

Dana explained her vision of creating a new book based on *Life Mapping* and she wanted to know if I would be supportive. Once I felt the passion and devotion she has for the process, my answer was a resounding "Yes!"

Dana's plan has been to make life mapping more accessible in our digitally driven world. Her success in leading workshops provided the experience needed to refine the process to help others move from reasoning with their beliefs to the action steps necessary to bring their lives into alignment with those very beliefs. Once we align our beliefs with our actions, a powerful transformation begins. Our lives become more fulfilling, and we have less stress and conflict in our lives. This removal of the conflicts in our lives is the heart of the process. Those conflicts cause untold losses of time, personal freedoms, and relationships. Instead of mistaking motion for achievement, we uncover the actions needed to reach our goals. We become more efficient, calmer, and much more productive. We learn to balance our lives so that our families share in the joy of the ride that is this life.

I am writing this foreword because I believe Dana is the person most qualified to update the *Life Mapping* process and bring it to the masses. She is successful, articulate, empathetic, organized, and willing to do whatever it takes to deliver a quality book and the workshops to support it, which will motivate others to believe they can finally have the lives they have dreamed of. Only an unselfish person with a love for others could make this happen. Dana is that unselfish person who desires to be part of the solution of helping others succeed. I applaud and support her effort to make life better for other people.

I am pleased to pass the torch to her. Every person wanting to live a more fulfilled life will find Dana's new book a valuable asset.

Bill Cohen
Pebble Beach, CA
October 2018

Introduction

Eighteen years ago, I was desperately searching for the meaning of my life. While I was scanning the bookshelves in the self-help section at Barnes & Noble, *Life Mapping* leapt into my hands. Its pale-yellow cover and intriguing title stirred my curiosity and immediately struck a chord with how I envisioned living my life: in complete alignment with the reasons I believe I'm alive in the first place.

Bill Cohen, the author of *Life Mapping*, offered a clear and easy-to-follow system for creating goals in a much more meaningful way than simply making a list—a way that greatly increased the odds of achieving my goals. Yet what drew me in were the three basic, yet very complex, questions he asked:

"What do you believe about how it all began—
our universe and humanity?"

"Why are you here living this life?"

"How do you want to show up in life?"

Bill insisted that the answers to these questions should be known *before* we write down our specific goals in life. His reasoning for this was simple:

We should only be pursuing goals that are in alignment with our fundamental belief system.

Life Mapping has transformed my life. It helps me reach for my full potential. It awakened me to the conflicts that prevent us from becoming the persons we were created to be. I came to understand that these conflicts exist because there are inconsistencies in what we believe, the way we think, and, ultimately, in our actions. These incongruencies confuse us, give us uneasy feelings, and prevent us from becoming the person we say we want to be. Our bodies don't lie, so when something is out of whack, we feel it on a cellular level. When the conflicts are gone, anxiousness fades away.

For me, the book was a journey of self-discovery that allowed me to truly let my light shine. I learned who I was, who I am, and how I want to show up in this world. To this day, Bill's process calls those of us who are stuck, who are afraid of failing, or who have played it safe to try something different—because if we don't, we know we'll continue to die inside.

A First Step

After I contacted Bill through Facebook, we set up a call. We talked for ninety minutes. He must have been a little taken aback. I gave him the in-depth background story on how his book helped to shape my focus over the past eighteen years. Bill couldn't have been more gracious, open, and willing to listen to me. He invited me to send him a detailed proposal outlining my idea.

I worked feverishly on the outline in between work, being a mom, shuttling to driver's ed, tutoring, sports practices, volunteering for high school football team dinners, and watching my sons play in their games. I tend to get caught in the weeds of the details, but I wanted it to be just right. Finally, three weeks later, I felt I had a substantive outline to send him. True to Bill's incredibly responsive communication style, he replied the next day telling me he was happy to support me and asked what I thought were the next steps.

It was important for me to meet Bill and his wife in person. I suggested flying to California, and they were kind enough to welcome me into their home. So, the week after Thanksgiving I flew into Monterey (one of the destinations I've had listed on my life map for years—check!) and spent time getting to know Bill and Gail.

Their hospitality was just as warm as he'd been toward me since the day I instant-messaged him with my bold idea. Bill and I sat for hours at his kitchen table talking about how Life Mapping came to be. He shared how it influenced his life and those of his children, wife, co-workers, and students. Beyond the obvious of providing direction and working to accomplish their goals, the book created a common language and way of living.

The three of us enjoyed a wonderful dinner at the Pebble Beach country club restaurant and inhaled the incredible Pacific Ocean view before sunset. Gail baked homemade scones for breakfast the next morning, and we all took a nice walk along the beach before it was time for me to leave.

Bill offered unwavering support as I endeavored to breathe new life into his creation. *Life Mapping* has inspired and sustained a vision of my future and countless others, and I am so grateful that he is graciously passing me the torch.

A Part of the Whole

So why my passion for Bill's book? Understanding who we are, who we can become, and how we fit into the world requires us to step back and look at the bigger picture. We need to understand that we are dependent upon the delicate balances in nature. We are dependent upon one another. If one small element, such as oxygen, were taken out of the mix, it would mean the end of humanity. We live in a time of "me, me, me," but if we stop, look around, and notice the incredible beauty and power of nature and the universe, it's easy to see that life is about so much more than us.

We must also think long range and globally. What will the long-term results be, generations into the future, of the world we are creating? No longer can one country or one continent ignore the rest of the world when planning its future. International organizations must learn to work together for the common good of all humanity. That will happen when enough individuals around the world unite behind a common cause. Governments are slow to change. Usually, change occurs only after a majority of the population *demands* it. Are you going to be part of the population that demands change?

The history of humanity is filled with leaders who championed great ideas. As you study these ideas, you begin to see a trend: Concern for the development of mankind was the theme that ran through their lives and teachings. Even though people's lives have improved as technology has evolved, the development of the human race still needs to be the primary focal point. Values such as honesty, loyalty, humility, and respect were stressed once upon a time and became the moral foundation of most societies. It was sometime in the mid-twentieth century that things began to change—seemingly when the pace of life began to quicken. People were suddenly forced to make more decisions in a single day than their parents had made in a month or their great-grandparents had made in an entire year.

The ideas that had grounded past generations began to blur when sound principles were no longer passed on from one generation to the next. Our newest generation is forced to deal with this ever-quickening pace without the benefit of learning to embody values that helped their ancestors make the tough choices that life forces upon us. The modern world focuses more on amassing possessions, looking good, being more efficient, appearing smarter, acquiring skills, or just plain winning at any cost. Since it doesn't appear there's an earthly force to slow this wave, we have a responsibility to turn inward to intentionally decide what we believe about our world and how we intend to show up in it.

I believe that this tidal wave is leading us away from our wiser self. As we begin to do whatever it takes to get ahead, most will deviate from the inner blueprint that guides us to our soulful calling. That inner blueprint has been given many names: consciousness, intuition, soul, spirit, karma, aura, core, or Tao.

This deviation creates a conflict. We no longer see ourselves as the person we had hoped to become. Each day we are less happy with the person we are becoming. We can no longer allow ourselves the time to think about the conflict because it is too painful. Our hearts ache, wondering, "Is this it? Is this my life?" That's unsettling because we know at our very core we were created for more. We are afraid to be alone with our thoughts, so we listen to music, disappear into other people's lives scrolling through our cell phones, surf the web, detach with addictions, watch television, immerse ourselves in work or play, sometimes all at once. Anything to keep our minds busy and distracted from the emptiness and disappointment we feel.

Will this continue to work? I don't think so. Our subconscious minds are still able to feel the disconnect, and we remain internally unsettled. We may have the big house, fancy car, and great job, or we may be on the brink of losing everything. Bottom line: Many of us aren't truly satisfied; we don't feel fulfilled. So we start looking for answers in all the wrong places. Some have affairs, divorce their partners, change companies, yell at the kids, start drinking, smoking, or popping pills—anything other than taking the time to feel the pain of not living a life connected to our God-given purpose here on earth. The answers lie within us. All we need to do is get quiet and listen. Find a quiet moment and ask yourself this question:

Am I satisfied with how I am living my life?

If the answer is "no," then this is your invitation to do something about it—now!

The Awakening

Shhh! Can you hear it, that inner voice that speaks to you? The sage voice full of wisdom well beyond your years that whispers in your ear? Do you believe he or she has your best interests at heart? Or do you turn a deaf ear because you can't begin to imagine how you would get from where you are today to where she wants you to go? What messages have you been hearing? Is something stirring deep inside? Will you acknowledge your intuition? Will you act? When you are ready, you will!

You are an amazing spirit! No one else has your unique gifts, traits, skills, abilities, and capacity for acquiring wisdom. You can do anything with these talents, but what will you do? To put the question another way: What is the most important thing you will do in your lifetime? Some might answer: successfully raise children, have an enjoyable career, find the cure for cancer, or explore life on Mars. All good answers. But what is most important to you? Are you already living your life aligned with what it is you say is most important or do you have some work to do to get there? If you do these things, will they bring you joy and deep satisfaction? If you die without doing them, will you feel regret? *Live Your Gift* is designed to help you achieve the life you are meant to live.

Marianne Williamson, an internationally acclaimed motivational speaker, spiritual teacher, and author, is a modern-day leader helping people find greater meaning in life. The opening poem in her *New York Times* bestseller *Return to Love* beautifully articulates the little positive, encouraging voice I'm training myself to listen to:

> "Our deepest fear is not that we are inadequate. Our deepest fear is that we are powerful beyond measure. It is our light, not our darkness that most frightens us. We ask ourselves, who am I to be brilliant, gorgeous, talented, fabulous? Actually, who are you not to be? You are a child of God. Your playing small does not serve the world. There is nothing enlightened about shrinking so that other people won't feel insecure around you. We are all meant to shine, as children do. We were born to manifest the glory of God that is within us. It's not just in some of us; it's in everyone. And as we let our own light shine, we unconsciously give other people permission to do the same. As we are liberated from our own fear, our presence automatically liberates others."

We feel a spark of magic when we live life in alignment with our God-given gifts. It's a feeling of pure joy derived from expressing what makes us unique. It's not hard, labored work; it's easy, like jumping on a bicycle and going for a ride. There's a feeling of confidence that we are living our journey on the right path, the path our souls are destined to live.

It's the feeling of authenticity.

When I discovered Bill Cohen's book, I knew I had found the means for life mapping my authentic life. But what I had to discover was my authenticity—that spirit unique to only me. I had to discover my gift.

To be honest, that can be hard work. The process requires you to look deep inside and sift through your strengths and weaknesses, your curiosities and fears, and your heartaches and joys—all those moments that have shaped your life and have brought you to where you stand today. It requires looking at your beliefs and principles and values, determining if they align with what you truly desire in life, and then weeding out what is stopping you from attaining your goals. What you will be left with after this process is your gift.

When I look around the world today, I see so many wonderful examples of people who are living their gift. No matter their chosen field—whether entertainment, sports, or business—their authentic lives shine brightly. Throughout this book, I would like to share some of those stories with you. They inspire me, and I know they will inspire you as well.

Mostly, what I hope these pages will help you do is the following:

- Understand what you believe about life and, specifically, why you're alive
- Create your own playbook for how you want to show up
- Identify your top five core values
- Learn to reconnect to what brings you joy
- Learn a system for setting, categorizing, and prioritizing goals
- Understand why it's important to align goals with beliefs, principles, and values
- Learn how to build a foundation for goals to increase the odds of success
- Discover efficiencies in scheduling and time blocking
- Understand the importance of implementing structure and accountability
- Learn how to drastically improve your opportunity of living a truly meaningful life

Throughout the book, you will see two icons. They signify the following:

The notebook icon refers to an exercise or activity to be completed in the *Live Your Gift Companion Guide*, a workbook that has been specially designed to accompany this book. The workbook allows for easy reference to the material contained herein. It is available from www.lifemappinginstitute.com, in book form or as a downloadable PDF. If you do not have the workbook, simply use a notebook.

The clipboard icon refers to Put It into Practice, a reference for how frequently you should review your goals and actions. A downloadable PDF Review Card is also available at www.lifemappinginstitute.com/resources.

This book was more than a labor of love for me, it was a gift to myself and others by honoring what I believe to be God's intention for me. I hope you find it a simple and systematic process for gaining clarity about who you are, what you believe, and where you want to go—and then go out and share your gift with the world!

Part One

live your gift

CHAPTER ONE

Your Gifts

> "Somebody should tell us, right at the start of our lives, that we are dying. Then we might live life to the limit, every minute of every day. Do it, I say! Whatever you want to do, do it now! There are only so many tomorrows."
>
> —Pope Paul VI

Living Their Gift

I want to share a story with you—one about a woman named Susan. Some of you may already know of her and will thus be able to understand why I chose her to open this book. For those of you who have not heard of her, the following short narrative of what transpired over the course of one magical night ranks among the most heartwarming stories of the last decade—and a beautiful example of believing in your gifts and chasing after an authentic life.

> It is April 11, 2009, and Susan takes the stage of a Glasgow, Scotland, theater. She is twice the age of many of the contestants competing with her on a British talent show, and the derisive whistles at her matronly appearance can be heard as she approaches the panel of judges seated below her in the auditorium.
>
> "What's the dream?" the lead judge asks.
>
> "I'm trying to be a professional singer."
>
> "And why hasn't it worked out so far, Susan?"
>
> "I've never been given the chance before, but here's hoping it'll change."
>
> "And who would you like to be as successful as?"
>
> "Elaine Paige," she responds.
>
> The judges' laughs are joined by countless snickers and harrumphs throughout the theater. And then the music plays, and she begins to sing . . .

Before the first verse was completed, Susan Boyle, an unassuming unemployed forty-seven-year-old from Blackburn, West Lothian, Scotland, had the audience on its feet screaming with joy and applauding wildly. The lead judge, the notoriously hard-hearted Simon Cowell, was stunned, as were his fellow judges Amanda Holden and Piers Morgan.

Within a week, Susan had become a worldwide sensation thanks to millions of YouTube views of the show.

For most of us, standing on a stage and hearing the jeers that Susan experienced would be enough to send us heading for the exit—to give up on our dream. But what endears Susan's story to so many is that she was used to such treatment. Misdiagnosed as having brain damage at an early age, she was constantly harassed at school and called "Susie Simple." (In 2012, she was diagnosed with Asperger's syndrome, a condition on the autism spectrum.) As an adult, she was labeled a reclusive spinster by neighbors, one who lived alone and sometimes did not surface from her home for long periods of time. And when she took the stage during *Britain's Got Talent*, she was immediately judged by her appearance.

Inside her, however, was a woman desiring to lead the life she believed could be hers, to share her incredible gift with the world—a voice comparable to that of Elaine Paige that has since helped her to perform all over the world, sell more than 25 million records, and achieve numerous awards and distinctions.

Susan Boyle faced many challenges over her life. She faced disapproval and ridicule on the stage that night. Today, however, because she believed in her gift, she is a professional singer loved by millions around the world. What perhaps is most fitting about her story and her journey to her authentic life is that it began that night in April 2009 with the song "I Dreamed a Dream."

“There are enough people in the world who are going to write you off. You don't need to do that to yourself.”

—Susan Boyle

Finding Our Gifts

Gifts are those special skills we have that allow us to do some things better than most other people. Think of the way Serena Williams plays tennis, Meryl Streep effortlessly speaks with foreign accents to portray characters, Ellen DeGeneres immediately puts her guests at ease, or Warren Buffett zeroes in on opportunistic investments.

At times, our gifts may be locked away, hidden by past trauma and pain, just waiting for the chance to shine, as in Susan Boyle's case. Lady Gaga has openly shared her story of being bullied; Mariah Carey has told of her struggles with bipolar disorder; and Janet Jackson has been honest about her battle with severe depression, all in the hopes of spreading awareness so that others in the same position may not feel so alone.

All of us have gifts. You might have always thought that you were without one. But think again, because everyone has at least one, and most have many. Try asking your friends, spouse, significant other, or siblings about your gifts. Think about the things you really don't mind doing, the things that come easily to you. We express our gifts effortlessly and naturally. We often take them for granted because we don't realize how lucky we are to have them. Others who don't possess them are keenly aware of their value. You might have to extract the common elements from several different activities before the picture becomes clear enough for you to see.

What do you admire most about the people closest to you? What traits are unique to your spouse, partner, children, or best friend? Whom do you call for help when your cable or internet access or your computer is acting up? Do you know someone who paints beautiful pictures, plays incredible music on the piano, or dances with grace? Who lifts you up with encouragement when you are feeling down? Whom do you turn to when you need a dose of honest advice? Who is the go-to handyperson who has an engineer's mind and can fix anything? A fabulous cook? Gardener? Everyone has a gift . . . everyone!

Your heart will overflow with satisfaction when you align your gifts with your purpose. When you live your life aligned, a flood of positive benefits follows. Contribution, accomplishment, fulfillment, growth, and happiness, just to name a few. You might think that some of the gifts that bring you and others joy are trivial, but nothing is trivial if it positively impacts others. Something as simple as telling stories to children might be your purpose. It may be the very reason you are here. You may be one special storyteller who brings a child's dreams to life.

My fifth-grade teacher, Mrs. Hall, had a purpose. It was to make every student she ever taught feel important, capable, and able to see the world through a bigger lens than our classroom portal. She didn't get paid to do this; she was paid to teach a specific curriculum. Not only did she manage to teach us the fifth-grade material, but she also gave us the gift of accomplishment and a belief that we could achieve great things. She radiated her passion every day, every time she saw us.

One of Mrs. Hall's curriculum requirements was for us to learn cursive writing. Oh boy, did we learn cursive! She inspired us to want to have elegant penmanship. Everyone rose to the level of beautifully composing fluid, rounded cursive letters to spell out "The quick brown fox jumped over the lazy dog's back." Why that sentence? Because it includes every letter of the alphabet!

She added a modest reward tied to excellence. Once she felt we had mastered the technique of graceful penmanship, we were awarded a *prized pen*. Every Thursday afternoon she administered the test and when Friday morning rolled around, we silently but eagerly chanted to ourselves, "Pick me, pick me." Her sparkling eyes and smiling face radiated pride the moment she called the next name on the list. I can still hear her excited sing-songy voice calling mine. "Dana Mellin!" Time froze as she celebrated my accomplishment. Standing beside me, keeping one arm wrapped around me in a side hug, she grabbed the special box off her desk and put it in my hands. I couldn't wait to undo the ribbon and hold my shiny new pen for the first time.

I can't help but tear up when I write about this because that's the magic of how expressing our gifts can touch others in a way they will never forget. Mrs. Hall's joy from living her gift was so pure it washed over us to the point it altered something inside. Some people confuse purpose and gifts with career. They might be somehow connected to your career as with Mrs. Hall. Teaching was just the vehicle she used to express her gift. Or it may be a gift you are here to share with others completely independent of how you pay your bills.

Mrs. Hall had the gift of drawing out the very best in her students. She developed students with confidence and fostered a belief we would all achieve our goals. While planting the individual seeds, she nurtured and "loved on" a classroom of children who were all growing in the same garden. Her gift of believing in us also taught us how to cheer on our friends, encourage them, and celebrate their successes, too. I have more friends from Mrs. Hall's fifth-grade class that I am still in touch with today than any other year in school.

Imagine if we all shared our gifts with each other. Our experience of life would be magical!

It's time to think about your personal gifts. What skills and abilities have you been blessed with? What comes easily to you? What tasks are you happy to do for others? Everyone has gifts and you should be proud of what you do well!

In the *Live Your Gift Companion Guide* or on an individual sheet of paper, list all the gifts, skills, and talents you believe you possess. Consider asking three to five of the closest people in your life what they see as your natural strengths and abilities.

CHAPTER TWO

Your Beliefs

> “Every now and again, you will feel a dull ache in your soul. A gentle humming around your heart. A longing for something without a name. If I ever told you to obey anything, this would be it. Listen to the call of your authentic self. That part of you that lives just outside of your own skin. Let it have its way with you. I have died a hundred times trying to ignore it.”
>
> —Mia Hollow

Living Their Gift

In 2008, Malala was just eleven years old when the Taliban took over her village of Swat Valley and banned education for girls, destroying 400 schools during their terror campaign. The following year, she was among more than 1 million people forced to leave their homes. Strong in her conviction that all girls should have the right to an education, she started an underground blog on the BBC to speak out against the Taliban.

At the age of fifteen, she courageously stood up to the Taliban regime, speaking publicly on behalf of girls in Pakistan. In doing so, she became a target, and in October 2012, a gunman boarded her school bus, asked for her by name, and proceeded to shoot her.

Malala was hit by three bullets, one of them entering and exiting the left side of her head and lodging in her shoulder. She was taken to a military hospital and then flown to England, where she was put into an induced coma for ten days.

Nine months later, after several skeletal and nerve-related surgeries, she returned to school.

Malala Yousafzai was just seventeen years old when she was awarded the Nobel Peace Prize in 2014. In receiving it, she stated, "This award is not just for me. It is for those forgotten children who want education. It is for those frightened children who want peace. It is for those voiceless children who want change."

That same year, the Malala Fund was established. It assists lobbying efforts in Afghanistan, India, Pakistan, Brazil, and Nigeria for gender equality, education for girls, education funding, teacher training, and, specifically, female teachers. It champions building schools, opposing forced marriage, and furthering the belief that all girls should be guaranteed twelve years of education.

Malala, now a student at Oxford University studying philosophy, politics, and economics, holds true to her belief in the fundamental principle of equal education for all. Her activism in fighting for the rights of women is inspirational and a beautiful example of living one's gift.

"Do not wait for someone else to come and speak for you. It's you who can change the world."

—Malala Yousafzai

Your Personal GPS

What we believe in and how we stand strong in our convictions are what make us authentic. Malala's beliefs moved her to action, even in the face of certain danger. We, too, must find the courage to move toward our individual purpose in life, even if that means facing fears that have previously held us back.

Our beliefs are at the core of who we are as human beings and form the foundation of life mapping. Confidently navigating through life requires a set of strong, sturdy beliefs. Each day we wake, and with every step we've taken since we first learned to walk, we wander deeper into uncharted territory. Every human life that has ever been or will ever be is an expedition of infinite possibility. Think about that. Not only are we the only person who looks like us, thinks like us, and acts like us on the entire planet, but our unique journey, every experience, emotion, and choice, is also ONE IN 7.6 BILLION!

It's powerful and awe-inspiring to realize the magnitude of the odds of you and me being born. It really is miraculous, isn't it? We're positioned at the helm of what will either be an adventure of a lifetime, weathering the perfect storm, or finding the calm after the storm. If you're like me and find yourself tossing about in the swells more than sailing on calm seas, I have good news: life mapping will provide you with a route toward smooth water.

Given the length of our journey, it seems prudent to put some thought into our aspirations for the future. For some, making it to the average lifespan of 76.1 years for men and 81.1 years for women seems like a nice, long life. For others, mortality and the thought of life ever coming to an end is scary. I'd like to assume if you're reading this book that you're interested in creating an amazing life for yourself no matter what the duration. Living a life where you're in control of your final destination begins with understanding your beliefs.

Beliefs are like the deep, gnarly, twisting, turning roots that anchor the biggest oak trees securely in place for hundreds of years. Roots form the base structure of a tree, but they are also interdependent on the other parts of the tree living healthfully to find harmony. Our beliefs allow us to live out our intended purpose. And, like roots dependent on other parts of the tree to flourish, our beliefs depend on our actions and character working together to support our most ideal self.

There are two parts to the belief question:

1. Discovering your beliefs about humanity in general
2. Understanding your individual beliefs

The universe, our planet Earth, and human life are complex and interdependent. Most people would live radically different lives if they unequivocally knew and believed without a shadow of a doubt that there was a distinct reason for their life. Unfortunately, most of us aren't guided or encouraged to explore the question. It may even seem like an impossible task. However, it is less complicated than you might imagine. How will knowing your beliefs change the way you live your life?

Beliefs drive every human behavior. Have you ever stopped to ask yourself why you think you're alive? It would be fascinating if people introduced themselves by their beliefs about life versus what they do for a living. We'd get to know each other on a much different level, wouldn't we? Well, I want to know what you believe about why you're living and I'm inviting you to carve out time to really consider the question.

If you create a well-defined Beliefs List and act upon it accordingly, you should be happy with your choices most of the time. Without a well-defined Beliefs List, you will find yourself living life in response to the needs of your environment and the people you interact with instead of proactively living your own desires and aspirations. In other words, if you don't know what you're doing here, you'll end up living life as defined by everyone other than you. The behavior associated with that life will reflect the combined influences of the people, places, and things trying to run your life for you.

Our attitudes are shaped by that which we truly believe. Without a clear idea of what we truly believe, we are like animals, and our attitudes are shaped by our environment. We abdicate control of our attitudes, and thereby our lives, to anyone willing to take the time to influence us. The act of writing down our beliefs is the first step in gaining control of our lives. Possibility begins to unfold once we're clear about our beliefs. We're born with an amazing ability to experience conscious thought and emotion. We have free will and the opportunity to live life to the fullest potential.

It's a Matter of Perspective

"What you see and hear depends a good deal on where you are standing; it also depends on what sort of person you are," reads a line from C. S. Lewis's *The Magician's Nephew*. This Lewis quote reminds me of a story. A man was sitting on a fence at the edge of a small western town in the late nineteenth century. A family in a wagon stopped to ask the man what kind of people lived in the town. The man asked about the kind of people the family experienced in their last town. The family replied that they left because most of the people were mean and cruel. The man responded by informing them that they would find the same kind of people in this town. Now, it might seem at first glance that the man was trying to discourage these people from moving into his town. A deeper look will reveal that the man was demonstrating one of the most solid principles of human interaction.

We, as humans, will find what we are looking for. If we look for the good in people, we will find it, and if we look for the bad in people, we will find it. The same people can often be seen from almost totally opposite points of view. This is the very point that Lewis makes. If we are to change the world we live in and the way people respond to us, we need to change the way we look at situations; we need to change our attitudes. Life mapping is a tool that will help us. The first step, the one that determines where we are standing, is developing our Beliefs List. Everything else is built on this foundation.

According to James Allen, known as the pioneer of the self-help movement:

> "What we are was designed and built by our own thoughts in our minds. If we nurture ignorant or evil thoughts, pain will soon follow. If our thoughts are healthy and beneficial, joy will follow us as surely as our shadows follow us on a sunny day. . . . Most of us are anxious to improve our circumstances but are unwilling to improve ourselves—and we therefore remain bound. If we do not shrink from the honest self-examination, we can never fail to accomplish the object upon which our hearts are set. . . . Law, not confusion, is the dominating principle in the universe; justice, not injustice, is the soul and substance of life; and righteousness, not corruption, is the molding and moving force in the spiritual government of the

world. This being so, we have to but right ourselves to find that the universe is right; and during the process of putting ourselves right, we will find that as we alter our thoughts towards things and other people, things and other people will alter towards us."

Your Individual Purpose

What is our purpose? Purpose—the reason one exists. *The reason one exists!* That is a rather sobering thought. It should be an exciting thought! Can you really have a purpose? You can, you do, and you wouldn't be here if you didn't. Parents, teachers, coaches, counselors, priests, ministers, and rabbis may help you discover your purpose, but they can't tell you what it is. Only you can discover it, uncover it, and own it! You will find it deep within your unique spirit. Not everyone has the same purpose. You are the only one who knows your true inner feelings and what is most meaningful to you.

Notice that I said meaningful, not pleasurable. Pleasure can be momentary, while meaningful actions provide a sense of fulfillment that is lasting. Fulfillment sends waves of positive, powerful energy throughout our body and beyond our physical self out into the universe. When we live aligned with our purpose, we will experience an ease that accompanies our actions.

Transform Pain into Purpose

Sometimes, the biggest obstacles we've overcome hold the key to our purpose. Whether heartbreak, trauma, or crisis, when we share our authenticity and vulnerability, we allow others access to healing. Have you ever noticed the most engaging speakers are those who also courageously share very personal details of their story? We are endeared to people who reveal their true selves. It doesn't matter if the pain was a result of poor choices, legal or illegal activity, or what we may label a shameful experience. I guarantee you the brutally honest speaker profoundly touches at least one person listening in the audience.

A lot of us walk through life pretending we're okay on the outside, while under the surface life is boiling in chaos. Everyone has a basic need for connection, and by offering our stories, we open a window to those still suffering by letting them know they're not alone.

The day I was born, I was blessed with the soul of a survivor. It's taken me forty-eight years to move toward sharing this gift more openly and publicly. Even those closest to me don't know all my darkest hours. When we vulnerably share, I believe we draw open the blinds on the windows to our soul. Spiritual authenticity is infinitely more powerful at connecting us than hiding behind our earthly restraints. Breaking free of our restraints once and for all allows us to reclaim our lives.

I've known for at least twenty-one years that God's ultimate intention for my life resides in something other than selling homes. It doesn't change the positive impact I've had or may continue to have through real estate. We still need to perform our jobs in line with our beliefs, principles, and values. I'm doubly blessed with a career I love and a belief God has more in store for me. My soulful wisdom's been whispering to me for years. Some years the voice was louder than others, but in the past few years the volume's been pegged on high. I simply couldn't ignore it any longer. She's pulling me in a direction where I am now finally surrendering and willing to follow her lead.

Our purpose may lead to another career, or it may not. The point I'm trying to make is life is so fragile. If there's something meaningful you're being called to do, please be courageous and explore it. Moving in a new direction is a choice and is as basic as one action step after the other. Just like a baby learning to walk, we become stronger with each step until the day we can run. You'll find your strength and power in time. For now, decide to allow life mapping to help you create a plan.

As I've grown into a successful businesswoman selling luxury new construction homes, I've also stepped into my passion for sharing how purposefully setting goals has brought clarity and direction to my life. I've wrestled victoriously through many challenges in my life and continue to train, practice, and work through other areas where I'm still healing.

Teaching life mapping blesses me with feelings of joy and fulfillment as I describe in this book. It's hard to match words with the specific feeling because words don't do the overall sensation justice. Today I know I'm a survivor and believe my story is meant to be shared. I believe stepping into my gifts and purpose honors God. I believe this part of my journey will be the pinnacle of my existence as a human being and what I'm meant to contribute to the world. Now I want you to discover what brings you joy and fulfillment!

How Did It All Begin?

I would like you to begin your Beliefs List by asking the most basic question of all: How do you think it all began? What do you believe? Could it be the work of God, the Big Bang, or another theory drafted to explain our existence? In 1994 a Gallup poll found that 96 percent of Americans believe in God. Of course, there are many different descriptions and names for God. Confusion between what science theorizes, the literal interpretation of the Bible, and church corruption has led people to abandon the question, in favor of faith, spirituality, or disbelief. Now the Gallup poll of 2016 stated that number is continuing to decline; it reported that 89 percent of Americans claim to be believers. Your work is to resolve the question to your own contentment. You can listen to the arguments on both sides, but in the end, you must decide what you believe.

Your idea of how life began will help you formulate your concept of the purpose of life in general, and eventually—with the knowledge of your passion, pains, gifts, what brings you true joy—of your individual purpose.

We can't wait for someone to come along and tell us how it all began or what they think our individual purpose is. We need to seek the answers ourselves. People will debate the merits of religion versus science for all of eternity, but, ultimately, what you need to ask yourself is: What do I believe? Regardless of a religious background or not, you can create a Beliefs List. Armed with your beliefs about the universe, you will be able to develop *your* personal Beliefs List about the reasons you think you're alive. The answers to these questions lie within each of us. The struggle comes from not slowing down long enough to hear the answers.

It's important that we have conviction so we can become the person we envision from our Beliefs List — the person we know at the core of our soul we are meant to be. We must be able to see ourselves fulfilling our purpose. Remember, at the end of our lives, it is our character and behavior that will define us. Wouldn't you rather be in control of your final destiny and know unequivocally that people experienced you as the person you intended to be? I know I do; I have faith you do, too!

Here is a good working definition of "belief" from *Merriam-Webster's Dictionary*:

> **Belief:** something that is accepted, considered to be true, or held as an opinion.

If you have the conviction and accept something to be true, it should be included in your list. Every time you add a new belief, ask yourself why you believe it. Your answer will lead you to deeper, more basic beliefs. The idea behind making a Beliefs List is to create a list that wholly encompasses your major beliefs. There is no correct number of beliefs. However, if a stranger reads your list, they should have a good sense of you, your idea of how it all began, what you think the purpose of humanity is, and your individual beliefs specifically.

Be patient with yourself, but not too patient. There is no reason to be in a hurry to create your list, but you also don't need to stay stuck because you're not sure. There are lots of probing questions ahead to help you figure out what you believe. Read articles, visit with people who might already have a well-defined Beliefs List, and take the time to think about the meaning behind the question. Most importantly, listen to that little voice in your head. It is your inner wisdom speaking to you.

Here is a sample of a thorough Beliefs List, also referred to as a personal credo, written by John D. Rockefeller Jr. (1874–1960):

> "***I believe*** in the supreme worth of the individual and in his right to life, liberty, and the pursuit of happiness.
>
> ***I believe*** that every right implies a responsibility; every opportunity, an obligation; every possession, a duty.
>
> ***I believe*** that the law was made for man and not man for the law; that government is the servant of the people and not their master.
>
> ***I believe*** in the dignity of labor, whether with head or hand; that the world owes no man a living, but that it owes every man an opportunity to make a living.
>
> ***I believe*** that thrift is essential to well-ordered living and that economy is a prime requisite of a sound financial structure, whether in government, business, or personal affairs.
>
> ***I believe*** that truth and justice are fundamental to an enduring social order.
>
> ***I believe*** in the sacredness of a promise, that a man's word should be as good as his bond; that character—not wealth or power or position—is of supreme worth.

> ***I believe*** that the rendering of useful service is the common duty of mankind and that only in the purifying fire of sacrifice is the dross of selfishness consumed and the greatness of the human soul set free.
>
> ***I believe*** in an all-wise and all-loving God, named by whatever name, and that the individual's highest fulfillment, greatest happiness, and widest usefulness are to be found in living in harmony with His will.
>
> ***I believe*** that love is the greatest thing in the world; that it alone can overcome hate; that right can and will triumph over might."

Note that Rockefeller stated his beliefs in a positive manner. There is no room for doubt in a belief. It is helpful to begin each belief with the words *I believe.* Until we understand our origin and our purpose, and develop a clear Beliefs List, we will be at the mercy of those who would influence us by default. Once you discover what *you* believe to be true, you'll possess a powerful compass from which to navigate your best life.

It's time to develop your Beliefs List. The following are some thought-provoking questions that may help you, as well as a list of beliefs taken from those submitted by participants in my Life Mapping Institute Workshops. They might give you some ideas as you create your own Beliefs List.

- What is something you say that encapsulates what you think about life? Example: No time like the present. All you have is today. Live life to the fullest.

- Do you consider yourself spiritual or religious?
- Do you believe in God or another Higher Power?
- Do you have a huge dream or goal you've been carrying around with you that sums up why you think you're here?
- Why are you able to feel emotions, have intellectual thoughts, and communicate with others?
- What is most important to you in your life?
- Do you have a spiritual practice? If so, what is it and where do you practice it?
- Do you have certain cultural beliefs or ceremonies you participate in?
- Is there something about Nature that is spiritual to you?
- What are your beliefs about food and how you nourish your body?
- What are your beliefs about your physical body, your vessel through life?
- Is family important to you? If so, why?
- Do you think you have a soul?
- What do you think happens to your essence or soul when you die?
- Do you believe in burial or cremation of your physical body?
- What do you love to do most?
- What are your most profound life-defining moments? Do they play into your beliefs at all?
- What do you fear?
- What are your beliefs about love, hate, and forgiveness?

Sample Beliefs

1. *I believe* people should associate and communicate with others; it's essential.
2. *I believe* a sense of humor can be one's greatest asset.
3. *I believe* all people are interconnected and therefore their decisions affect other people.
4. *I believe* all people deserve respect.
5. *I believe* all people have the capacity to love and accept others.
6. *I believe* all people have the right to speak their mind.
7. *I believe* all people possess the capacity to do good.
8. *I believe* beauty is relative.
9. *I believe* challenging oneself to higher, more difficult levels is the path to finding yourself.
10. *I believe* education leads to better decisions.

Activity

- In the *Companion Guide* or on an individual sheet of paper, take some time to record your concept of the universe's existence. After you have your concept about the universe, write a statement in which you describe your concept of the purpose of life in general.
- Next, write down your list of personal beliefs.

Before moving on, take one more sweep through your beliefs and ask yourself whether the beliefs you have written down are truly representative of your beliefs or default beliefs that belong to someone else who influenced you. If so, that's perfectly fine if you also truly believe them. The idea here is to be sure you own what you've included in your Beliefs List. This list is yours and yours alone. Make any adjustments necessary and you'll be ready to move on. Some workshop participants felt this was the hardest part of their life map. If you end up feeling that way, too, then I want to really acknowledge your pushing through to complete your list.

Hopefully, this process has sparked insight into your purpose. You may have one idea to list, there may be several, or you may not be completely clear on what it is yet. That's okay and quite common. As we make our way through the rest of the book, hopefully you'll have additional revelations. Leave yourself open to the possibilities and ask the universe to give you a sign.

In the *Companion Guide* or on an individual sheet of paper, write down your purpose.

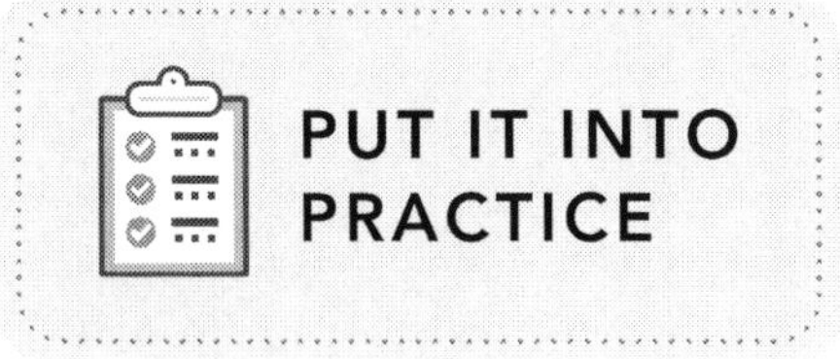

CHAPTER THREE

Your Principles

> "Live so that when your children think of fairness and integrity, they think of you."
>
> —H. Jackson Brown Jr.

Living Their Gift

She was born into extreme poverty, the daughter of an unwed teenage mother who left shortly after her birth. For six years she was raised by her maternal grandmother, Hattie Mae, an impoverished woman living in rural Mississippi who resorted to making her granddaughter dresses fashioned from potato sacks.

At the age of six, she moved into a Milwaukee ghetto with her mother; however, within two years she was sent off to live with her father. While she did return to Milwaukee, she was eventually sent away by her mother for good after she began stealing money.

The thefts stemmed from the ridicule she endured for being poor. This cruel mockery by the more affluent schoolchildren was reminiscent of the teasing by the local children back in Mississippi who had made fun of her potato sack dresses. Poverty was just one of the issues that impacted her during those formative years; the other had a much greater effect on her psyche.

From the age of nine through her early teenage years, she was sexually abused by men her family had trusted, including a cousin, an uncle, and a family friend. The abuse caused her to run away at the age of thirteen. A year later she found herself pregnant; she lost the child, a son who was born prematurely and died shortly after birth. When her father, Vernon, told her the baby had died, he said it was a "second chance" for her, and that became her mantra. "I was, in many ways, saved by that, and I made a decision that I was going to turn it around."

And she did. With Vernon providing the structure, discipline, and high expectations to drive her, she won a full scholarship to Tennessee State University. As a sophomore in college, she was hired by a local Nashville radio station to read the news. Then a CBS affiliate came calling, and she became Nashville's first African-American female co-an-

chor of the evening news. She moved to Baltimore to host a morning talk show and then to Chicago to serve as anchor for the last-place *A.M. Chicago* morning talk show. Less than two years later, after a successful climb in the ratings, the program was renamed *The Oprah Winfrey Show*.

Today, Oprah Winfrey is estimated to be worth $2.8 billion. She is one of the most respected, recognizable, and beloved women in the world. She has been named the most influential woman and the most influential black person of her generation by *Life*. Both CNN and Time.com have called her the world's most powerful woman. In fact, her opinions are so influential that "The Oprah Effect" has led to the success of authors (think Oprah's Book Club) and personalities (think Dr. Oz and Dr. Phil).

Oprah's gifts have extended well beyond talk show host. She has received critical praise for her acting in such films as *The Color Purple* and *Beloved* and has found success as a television producer and magazine publisher. She is also widely recognized as one of the greatest philanthropists of our time, giving away nearly half a billion dollars to educational causes and millions more through Oprah's Angel Network.

But it is the gift of gently reaching inside people to get at their story that has always been Oprah's greatest gift. First practicing those skills on her corncob doll back at Hattie Mae's, she has gone on to interview the most significant people of our time, sharing their stories to help us all deepen our understanding of ourselves and the world.

> "The whole point of being alive is to evolve into the complete person you were intended to be."
>
> —Oprah Winfrey

Rules for Life

As Oprah has taught us, it is not where you begin in life that shapes our existence but how you meet the challenges and step up to the opportunities offered. What has endeared her to so many people around the world is that she is truly authentic—open and honest about her past struggles and filled with a love for others and a desire to see them achieve greatness. The principles that she lives by set an example for us to see that before we can make a difference in the lives of others, we must first make a difference in our own. And that means identifying the principles by which we choose to live.

Principles are the bedrock of civilization; they serve to guide how we co-exist in the world, how we connect with one another, and, most importantly, how we treat each other. Without them, chaos would reign, and the fundamental rights of individuals would be diminished by those aiming to dominate and discriminate.

Fairness and integrity are examples of two principles. As you travel the road of life, you will need to know which rules to follow. Principles are your rules for life, your personal playbook, your inner GPS, and the behaviors you have chosen to live by and want to follow. How do you know which principles you should choose? The goal of identifying principles is to remove conflict.

There are certain laws and principles that exist in nature; gravity is an example. You can't change it, and it would be foolish to live your life trying to ignore it. There are also societal laws, like not driving the wrong way down a one-way street. Doing so would create conflicts that could cause you and others great physical harm. Your Principles List should include all the rules that you feel you need to follow to live your life in alignment with your Beliefs List. Your Principles List describes how you want to show up in the world for yourself and others.

Is there a perfect list of principles? I don't think so. Your goal is to develop your own list and continually refine it. Observe your actions over time and you will learn which principles to add, delete, or modify. Why can't you just take someone else's list? You can, but then you'd be living according to their rules. In order to reach alignment with yourself, you need a list that accurately describes who you are. When your beliefs, principles, and actions are in alignment, you will be well on your way to achieving your goals. You can always test one of your principles by asking yourself if society would be able to prosper with the opposite principle. For example, if honesty is on your list, ask whether society would be able to prosper with dishonesty as one of its core principles. If the answer is "no," then your principle is a sound one.

Why do we need to have rules? According to Tom Landry, one of the most successful and highly respected men to ever coach in the National Football League: "Most successful football players not only accept rules and limitations but, I believe, they need them. Players are free to perform at their best only when they know what the expectations are, where the limits stand." Landry's observation is correct. Our children clearly demonstrate this need. They continually test the limits of their environment until they understand them and feel the safety and comfort of those limits.

Laws are designed as boundaries to help set limits, to provide a sense of safety for citizens, and to help keep order. Unfortunately, many of our current laws in the U.S. are not adequately protecting innocent people. Frequent school shootings and other mass shootings are desensitizing all of us. This is a clear indicator of when laws need an overhaul, and we need to better address issues surrounding the mental health of people who commit these crimes. Senseless deaths should always be a call to action!

The enormity of what is unjust in our society and world is overwhelming. Some days after watching the news I feel helpless, but I remind myself I can only do what I can do. And, sadly, the reality is that I can't fix it all. What I can do is determine how much of the news I can healthfully consume. When I am healthy, I can contribute to others and focus on my passions in order to give back and effect change.

One of the best solutions to making a difference is focusing on ourselves first. Knowing your own limits allows you to live your life within them, resulting in less drama and a healthier life. The alternative is acting and reacting to the push and pull of all the other influences. Others' rules may not come close to aligning with yours, so watch out! Be the driver of your life rather than a passenger.

Benjamin Franklin made mastering principles his lifelong project. He called them virtues. Franklin understood that reaching perfection is an arduous task but that ignoring the labor leads to habits (lured by inclination, custom, or the company of others) that are self-destructive.

Here is an example of a quality Principles List, belonging to Franklin.

"1. **Temperance:** *I will* eat not to dullness. *I will* drink not to elevation.
2. **Silence:** *I will* speak not but what may benefit others or myself. *I will* avoid trifling conversation.
3. **Order:** *I* will let all my things have their places. *I will* let each part of my business have its time.
4. **Resolution:** *I will* resolve to perform what I ought. *I will* perform without fail what I resolve.
5. **Frugality:** *I will* make no expense but to do good to others or myself; i.e., waste nothing.
6. **Industry:** *I will* lose no time. *I will* be always employed in something useful. *I will* cut off all unnecessary actions.
7. **Sincerity:** *I will* use not hurtful deceit. *I will* think innocently and justly; and, if I speak, speak accordingly.

8. **Justice:** *I will* wrong none by doing injuries or omitting the benefits that are my duty.
9. **Moderation:** *I will* avoid extremes. *I will* forbear resenting injuries so much as I think they deserve.
10. **Cleanliness:** *I will* tolerate no uncleanness in body, clothes, or habitation.
11. **Tranquility:** *I will* be not disturbed at trifles or at accidents common or unavoidable.
12. **Chastity:** *I will* rarely use venery but for health or offspring—never to dullness, weakness, or the injury of my own or another's peace or reputation.
13. **Humility:** *I will* imitate Jesus and Socrates."

It's important to understand that the goal is to become the best you can be, not to reach perfection. Sometimes the challenge in achieving the most meaningful goals causes people to shun the idea, withdraw from even trying, and, eventually, develop defense mechanisms that ultimately become self-destructive. Unattained aspirations, especially those we know align with our core and purpose, will most likely leave us feeling incomplete or, worse, regretful.

Principles are signposts that we will use to make decisions when we come to forks in the road. The principles we select will determine the way we think, act, and react to everything in life. They anchor our actions and reactions as we move through life and provide context for our most ideal behavior. If aligned well with our beliefs, they provide feedback to us if we find ourselves operating outside our ideal behavior. Our souls will nudge us when this happens, guaranteed.

A lot of people ask me what the difference is between a belief and a principle. Beliefs refer to the *whys,* the reasons for doing things in life. Principles refer to the *hows*, the ways in which we do things. Principles are the guides we follow before we commit to things and the way we respond in everyday life. Beliefs are the reasons we follow our principles. If one of my beliefs is the Golden Rule, I could select the principle "I will not steal." That principle would be supported by my belief, since I do not want anyone to steal from me. Without the belief to support the rule, I would steal whenever it was to my benefit.

On your list you may have selected reliability as one of your principles. If so, when you start thinking about doing something, you will make sure it does not conflict with something else you have already committed to do. When you commit to doing something, people can count on you not only to be there but also to be on time. If someone points out to you that you are late, you no longer get mad at them for their observant remark but rather thank them and apologize for your tardiness.

Think of yourself walking on the path of life. Your Principles List is like a shield that protects you from people and events that will come along and attempt to push you off your path. The temptations that would have otherwise diverted you from your path are too weak to penetrate the shield. The farther along the path you travel, the stronger your shield becomes. One day, your core beliefs and your daily behaviors will be completely aligned. No longer will others be able to negatively influence you. No longer will your conscience battle for your attention because you will already be acting in a manner true to yourself. You will now be living up to your personal standards. That will be the day when you know your life map is making a positive difference in your life.

Responsibility

You can't delegate your responsibility for keeping your actions in alignment with your principles. You are responsible for your actions. It is possible for others to help you in your efforts to improve. Sharing your principles with caring friends and family, or an accountability partner, puts them in a position of giving you feedback. When they gently mention that your actions may conflict with your ideal behavior, you then have the opportunity to make the necessary adjustments. Ultimately, you will consciously choose your actions and thus define the person you are; however, help from caring friends and family will speed up the process.

Principles, with repetitive action and practice, will become habits. When a principle behavior is so ingrained into your personality that you would not knowingly or willingly violate it, it has become a natural response. Some of us need help with structure to practice these ideal behaviors. There are many ways to do this, but ultimately, you will need to decide what works best for you to stay on track with your list. Daily check-ins, reviewing your lists, and setting calendar reminders are helpful if you're working toward a noticeable shift.

Work to improve your thoughts; they ultimately lead to your behavior.

> "The thought manifests as the word;
> The word manifests as the deed;
> The deed develops into habit;
> And habit hardens into character;
> So watch the thought and its ways with care,
> And let it spring from love
> Born out of concern for all beings . . .
> As the shadow follows the body,
> As we think, so we become."
>
> —From the Dhammapada,
> Sayings of the Buddha

Character is built off what we do, not what we say we will do. Putting your ideal virtues into practice, even if they are not second nature initially, will ultimately influence how others perceive and experience you. Benjamin Franklin rotated the thirteen principles on his list every month. He also shared his list with a friend who helped him add to it. Only Franklin can describe the addition:

> "My list of virtues contained at first but twelve. But a Quaker friend having kindly informed me that I was generally thought proud, that my pride showed itself frequently in conversation, that I was not content with being in the right when discussing any point, but was over-bearing and rather insolent—of which he convinced me by mentioning several instances—I determined endeavoring to cure myself if I could of this vice or folly among the rest, I added Humility to my list, giving an extensive meaning to the word. I cannot boast of much success in acquiring the reality in this virtue, but I had a good deal with regard to the appearance of it."

Each month he recorded his actions involving that month's principle. He continued the process for over fifty years. He lived these virtues!

Honesty

Honesty includes being honest with ourselves. According to thought leader Bryant McGill, "Real transformation requires real honesty. If you want to move forward—get real with yourself!" This simple statement speaks volumes. Don't live by someone else's rules; develop your own personal playbook and live by it! Every time one person does this, there is one less person being influenced by someone who hasn't set their own moral compass right. Destructive behavior is more acceptable if large numbers of people are involved. The smaller the percentage of the population demonstrating such behavior, the more conspicuous they become. We can all be part of the solution to a kinder world if we take an honest look at ourselves first.

Here is a simple definition of a "principle" according to *Merriam-Webster's Dictionary*:

> **Principle:** a rule or code of conduct, habitual devotion to right principles.

If you believe that a principle should be followed and is supported by one or more of your beliefs, you should add it to your Principles List. For the sake of clarity, identify the belief or beliefs that support each of the principles on your list. You can consider your list complete when you can point to one of your beliefs as the guiding force in every major decision you have ever made and can conceive of making in the future.

It is recommended we begin each principle with the words *I will*. Aim for wording all your principles positively. Consider what you will do rather than what you will not do. Positive statements are more powerful motivators. Rather than depriving yourself, you will be taking charge of your life. There will be times when you will feel compelled to use the "not" word; referring to the use of alcohol might be one of those times. Instead, rebuild the principle to a positive statement; for example, I will live an alcohol-free life.

Famous singer Queen Latifah says, "It's not always easy to do the right thing. But doing the right thing makes you strong, it builds character, it forces you to make decisions based upon your beliefs and not what other people think. In life, and in business, you have to stand for what you believe in and sometimes you have to stand alone. But what makes you a leader is having the courage of your convictions."

Having a written list helps us remember what's important and how we want to show up. How many principles should you have? As many as it takes to provide you with a playbook for dealing with all the major decisions in your life. Remember, each principle should be supported by one or more of your beliefs.

It's time to develop your Principles List. On the next page you'll see some thought-provoking questions that may help you formulate your list. There's also a list of examples of principles supplied by participants from Life Mapping Institute Workshops.

Here are some additional questions to ask yourself:

- How do you connect and show love to those you care about?
- Do you have a responsibility to the environment?
- What do your best efforts look like toward work?
- How do you take care of your emotional health? Mental health? Physical health?
- How do you think you should optimally nourish your body?
- Which hobbies do you enjoy?
- How do you care for your overall health?
- How do you practice your religion? Spirituality? Time in nature?
- Are there parameters you have around money and the handling of it?
- What commitments are important for family?
- Is personal growth important to you? How will you continue to learn and grow?

- Is business or career growth important to you? How will you expand in this area?
- Is contributing to society important to you? If so, how do you like to lend a hand?
- Do you have hopes for traveling and exploring our country or world?
- Is there a specific contribution you are meant to make?
- How do you specifically handle conflicts? What would you want others to say about how you handle such conflicts? Are you fair, quick to apologize, do you own your part?
- What do your kids, friends, or family see you doing on a consistent basis?

Sample Principles

1. *I will* live with integrity, especially when most unpopular.
2. *I will* accept responsibility for my actions.
3. *I will* be a good listener with my spouse and kids.
4. *I will* care for my body by exercising regularly.
5. *I will* acknowledge and help others maximize their capacity to do good.
6. *I will* allow myself to make mistakes and will learn from them.
7. *I will* always be there for my family.
8. *I will* always keep improving myself.
9. *I will* seek to understand before being understood.
10. *I will* be an example of the value of hard work.

Before moving on, take one more sweep through your Principles List. I'd like you to consider the following questions: Do you believe all items on your list support how you'd like to show up in life? Are all the principles on your list guidelines you can claim as your own or are they someone else's expectations of you? If they belong to someone else, do you really want them on your list? If not, get rid of them. Are you out of touch with any of your principles? Are you acting inconsistently with what you have written down? If so, put a star next to the item. This will help you make a mental note for when we are working on goals. You can ask yourself if it's important to incorporate any goals to reconnect with those principles. This list is yours and yours alone. Make any adjustments necessary and then you'll be ready to move on.

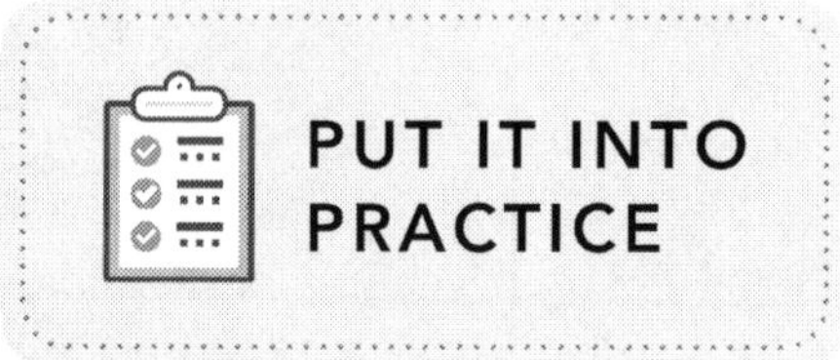

A Grateful Heart

Let's celebrate the goodness we experience in life. So often, we get so caught up in the frenzy of work, financial pressure, family responsibilities, relationships, the current local or national crisis, or our own crisis that we forget to stop and acknowledge what is going well. More importantly, when we take the time to express our gratitude toward another it pays high dividends. Scientific studies provide strong evidence that expressing gratitude (and it doesn't even have to be shared with the person—for example, journaling or writing letters but not sending them) elevates our overall sense of well-being. An article by Joel Wong and Joshua Brown, "How Gratitude Changes You and Your Brain," says that gratitude's positive impacts include "greater happiness, positive emotions, improved health, ability to deal with adversity, and building stronger relationships."

One study by Dr. Art Markman, shared in *Psychology Today*,

observed 300 adults, mostly college students, who described themselves as experiencing anxiety and depression. All participants were also enrolled to work with a counselor at the same time. The participants were split into three groups. One group was asked to write one letter of gratitude to another person once a week. The second group was asked to write about their negative emotions, and the third didn't write any letters at all. The data revealed significant increases in the participants' feelings of well-being for the group who wrote the letters. Benefits were noticeable at four weeks, but results at 12 weeks were even more positive.

It's a great reminder to intentionally pause, not only to be thankful for what we have, but also to welcome more appreciation and kind thoughts into our hearts and minds. A gratitude journal is a fabulous tool to become aware of what we're thankful for.

Two years ago, I started one, as suggested by one of my accountability partners, Cheryl. She had been journaling about her gratitude for at least a year and I was struck by her increased positivity. No matter what struggles she faced, tears she shed, or fears she carried, she had an amazing ability to snap out of her murky thoughts and remind Brandi (our other accountability partner) and me it was all going to be okay. She'd say, "I'm just going to continue to remind myself of all the wonderful things in my life. Today, I wrote about my love for my husband and my boys and that keeps me going."

Cheryl was diagnosed with breast cancer last year. She lost all her hair within a month of starting chemotherapy, she was terribly nauseated after treatments, and yet her attitude remained upbeat. She promptly purchased a beautiful, spunky new hairpiece and sauntered into our weekly meeting sporting it. She wore a look of courage, even though I'm sure she felt self-conscious. Cheryl leads by example. She focuses on her gratitude, lives for today, and has faith in her future. Her strength blows my mind!

In the *Companion Guide* or on a sheet of paper, write down some ways you are willing to practice gratitude. There are countless ways to express gratitude, but here are a handful of ideas to help you come up with your own.

Expressions of Gratitude

- Write in a gratitude journal
- Write letters of gratitude (send them or hold onto them)
- Write thank-you notes to people to express your gratitude
- Tell someone in person your gratitude for them
- Say thank you
- Spend quality time with someone you feel especially grateful for
- Decorate a special container or box for someone you want to show your appreciation to. Write a daily gratitude on a slip of paper and then give the container to the person. This one is great to save for Valentine's Day, Christmas, an anniversary, or other special occasion to express your gratitude. This is also great to do for your kids.
- Volunteer for an activity that shows your gratitude for nature
- Log your gratitude in a gratitude app

Acts of Kindness

Kindness—a simple action, yet how many of us purposefully go out of our way to show genuine kindness toward another human being? I'm not talking about the common courtesy of holding the door for others (however, more of that is always good), or saying, "Bless you" when someone sneezes (which is a nice thing to say). Rather, I'm referring to what we hear others refer to as "paying it forward" and actual "intentional acts of kindness."

What if we selected one day each week to do something kind for another? Whether that is buying a coffee for the person behind you at the Starbucks drive-through, picking up the tab of a person or family eating at a restaurant, or dropping off fresh food at a shelter, wouldn't it feel good to give kindness on a regular basis? Sibok Corbett Miller, who taught martial arts to all four of my boys, deserves a lot of credit for teaching the value of kindness to thousands of kids.

Sibok trained my boys from the time they were three years old all the way until each earned his black belt. (One of them until he earned his first-degree black belt.) The boys spent an average of three hours a week with Sibok, forty-eight weeks a year, for a total of at least eight years. In other words, Sibok coached 1,152 hours with each of my boys, for a total of 4,608 hours of teachable moments! That's the equivalent of hiring one full-time employee for two years! Sibok's philosophy isn't one of military-style discipline or competitiveness. However, they all learned enviable moral discipline, perseverance, and achievement, and all are genuinely respectful. Sibok's approach is one of kindness—teaching life-building skills through practical application and fostering honorable character.

One of the many weekly practices for students at Miller's Martial Arts is to complete training worksheets. Students have an opportunity to earn special stars for their uniforms when they do. One specific exercise is the "Random Acts of Kindness" worksheet. It came home with fifty empty boxes on it. Sibok expects the students to offer fifty good deeds to others, and standard chores do not count. Once the worksheet is filled up, the kids bring it to the studio in exchange for a red star. Students proudly wear their Gis (karate uniform) with stars prominently displayed.

Years later, this got me thinking about my habits regarding random acts of kindness. I decided to make a list of people who made a special impact on my life in a positive way. My first list included the branch manager at my local bank; the eyeglass store technicians; a handful of coaches who trained the boys in football, baseball, and soccer; and several parents who went above and beyond by treating my boys generously to special ski getaways, endless playdates, and fast-food stops after sporting practice. It was fun. It felt good to recognize how many people acted selflessly for the boys and me.

Those little acts of kindness are important to me, and I enjoy giving handmade gifts. Life is often hectic as a single mom working a full-time job (plus the usual extra hours). It would be easy and probably understandable for me to run in and grab a ready-to-go pastry box from Safeway's 24/7 bakery and stick a bow on top. I place a high value on my limited free time. But I feel like a homemade creation more accurately reflects my deep level of appreciation toward these amazing people.

One of life's simple pleasures for me is baking. (We'll be talking about this more in the next chapter.) I find it relaxing, satisfying, and a little therapeutic. It brings me joy to bake treats like cookies, pies, and cupcakes. Many times, one or more of the boys will gladly jump in to help. We package them up in fancy cellophane and cheerful ribbons and top them off with a homemade card or gift tag. If the gift is going to a family of one of my son's best friends or a coach, then my son will write a personal message in the card as well.

There's no better feeling, to me, than delivering these gifts as a way of saying "thank you!" The day I walked into my bank and handed Karla, the branch manager, a special gift and extra cookies for her staff, she was blown away. It felt so good to see her genuine appreciation for being recognized. I encourage you to think about people in your life who have taken good care of you. Whether it's the counter person at the dry cleaners, a favorite grocery clerk, or a hairstylist who makes you feel extra pretty or handsome. The simplest things often mean so much to others. Ultimately, we fill our heart and soul when we illuminate someone else's great character. Randomly acknowledging others who make a positive impact in our lives starts a positive, contagious ripple effect.

The front cover of *Live Your Gift* depicts exactly what I mean by ripple effect. Unique, beautifully formed concentric circles ripple with radiant energy when we *nail* our highest intentions. Authentically living in complete alignment with who we are and sharing that goodness with others allows us to leave a special impression that sends positive waves of energy out into the universe.

Spread the Love

When you are rushing on to your next goal, excited at the successful completion of your current one, remember to appreciate the people who have helped you along the way. Look for ways to give back to your community, your family, and your friends. This is a great opportunity to connect with those around you whom you love.

Memories of my younger childhood are sparse. With five kids, my parents had a tough time making ends meet and they didn't exude a whole lot of joy. They were under stress constantly and I think it mostly consumed their lives. Fun times exist only in a few vivid memories. There's one in particular that I'd like to share.

My dad has a passion for boats. Right after he graduated from college, he took a job in Alaska working for the Department of Fish and Game. His dad had been an avid fisherman and hunter, and he passed that love on to my dad. Once, when I was about five years old, my dad drove me to Sausalito, California, to walk the docks at the wharf. I couldn't tell you what was said; however, I knew it was his happy place. I remember being terrified at the sight of hundreds of crabs piled on one another inside a massive cardboard tote. They hissed and clawed as they awaited their fate. This was also my first instruction in the various types of fishing boats and the gear they used to catch fish like purse seiners, gill netters, trawlers, long liners, and crabbers.

In hindsight, I know it must have been bittersweet for my dad walking along the old creaking wooden boards nailed into the support pilings. He lost the two boats he owned when the herring industry went bust in 1974. However, the time he spent with me in Sausalito and one other day at Seattle Fisherman's Terminal etched a distinct love in my heart for all things water, docks, boats, crab, and fish. Even if unspoken, his profound respect for the force and beauty of nature and admiration for hardworking fisherman was clearly conveyed. He shared a piece of what he loved with me, and before I knew what had happened, at age nineteen I was working on a processing ship in the Aleutian Islands for five years.

As my dad demonstrated, we are all teachers, whether we realize it or not. What people learn from us is a function of our willingness to share ourselves and true passions. The things we love, and our observable behavior, is contagious; this can be for both good and bad. It is a rather large responsibility. Few experiences in life equal the joy of successfully mentoring another person. Both participants in the mentoring process are enriched. Whether the person you are mentoring is your own child or a complete stranger, the rewards are everlasting.

We should take whatever time is required to make sure everyone in our family understands the extent of our love for them. Wouldn't it be wonderful if those we care about most said, "My mom (dad, brother, sister, etc.) made a point of letting me know just how much she loved me." Sharing this with someone outside your family is the next step. Even though our friends list may number in the hundreds, people are hiding in plain sight feeling unloved, disconnected, and alone.

Consider all the people who have taken the time to help you in ways you never expected. Make a list of people you would like to show a random act of kindness. Their kind deeds may have taken place in the last week or it could be something from years ago still worthy of acknowledging. In the case of Sibok, his investment in the boys and my family is so meaningful that I think it's appropriate to pop in with a surprise more than once. If I'm recalling fond memories or feeling thankful, then doing something genuine and kind comes naturally. When it's heartfelt, we should share our true feelings, so they know how they've positively impacted our life.

It's also nice to share kindness with someone you don't know. These are totally random acts. Here is a list to springboard from. Add your personality and share things that are meaningful to you.

Random Acts of Kindness

- Bake cookies, cake, cupcakes, pie, bread
- Make a card for someone instead of buying one
- Pick up litter on your street
- Take someone flowers and surprise them
- Help a neighbor rake their leaves in the fall
- Offer to take a photo
- Offer to babysit for a friend
- Buy movie tickets for the people in line behind you
- Leave a kindness rock you've made for a friend or co-worker on their desk
- Compliment your restaurant server to their manager; better yet, send the manager a note about it or post a great review online
- Share an inspirational book with someone
- Say "I love you" to someone you love
- Write a note of thanks to a coach who has positively influenced your child
- Buy a supply of coloring books and crayons and give them to your friends' kids when they come over or to clients' kids at work
- Bring your neighbor's garbage can up the driveway for them
- If you see a parking meter expiring soon, put some coins in it
- Leave an extra-large tip for great service
- Talk to someone who seems alone at a party
- Post free items on a local community Facebook page

- Call your parents, grandparents, and siblings and tell them you love them
- Say thank you or give a gift to a janitor or maintenance person in your office building or at a school
- Take a warm dinner or dessert to your local fire station
- Give away a prepaid car wash

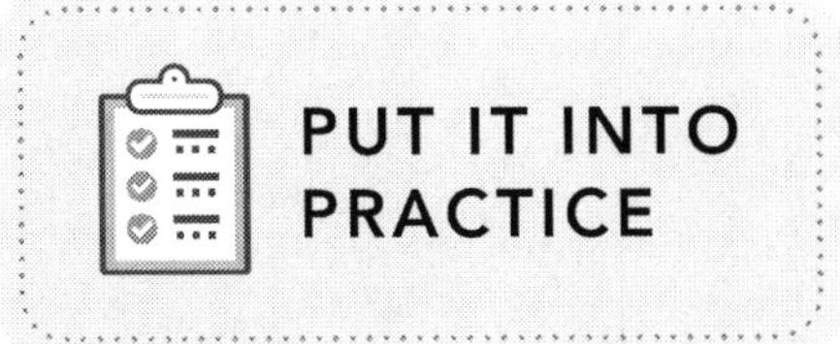

CHAPTER FOUR

Your Values

> “When your values are clear to you, making decisions becomes easier.”
>
> —Roy E. Disney

Living Their Gift

Walter's father was a stern and hardworking man who never could quite understand his son's fascination with art. In fact, he did not consider Walter's chosen profession—illustrator and artist—as having any real meaning and certainly not a real job.

However, Walter had a vision, and even though he did not have his father's support, he forged ahead, working as an apprentice artist at a commercial art studio. When he was laid off, he and his friend decided to open their own commercial arts business. It subsequently failed, and Walter joined a film ad company that made commercials using cutout animation.

While his interest in cutout animation grew, what truly fascinated Walter was a technique called cel animation, which allowed for repetition of images across frames instead of just flat images. He began experimenting with it and, convinced it was the better technique, began a new business making short cartoons. The company did achieve modest success, even growing into a full-fledged studio, but it fell into bankruptcy. Once again, Walter was left to start over.

This time, he left the Midwest and headed for California. Five years later, his creation of Mortimer Mouse—renamed Mickey by his wife, Lillian—appeared in the film short *Steamboat Willie.*

Walt Disney, the recipient of thirty-two Academy Awards, failed his way to success. How he succeeded was through perseverance and determination; but *why* he succeeded can be attributed to one thing: Walt had very clear values. Although he and his father had a tense relationship, Walt put family first, and he would not let the setbacks of previous ventures derail his dream of creating entertainment that would appeal to families.

Disney Brothers Studio, formed with his brother Roy, eventually moved away from cartoon shorts to feature-length cartoons, the first

of which was *Snow White and the Seven Dwarfs*. *Fantasia*, *Pinocchio*, and *Cinderella* were among the classics that followed, and today the Walt Disney Company continues to churn out classics like *Frozen*, adored by children and parents alike.

Walt's crowning achievement, however, was the creation of "The Happiest Place on Earth." In the early 1950s, he envisioned a theme park that would cater to families, especially children. Disneyland opened to visitors in July 1955, attracting nearly 3.5 million guests in its first year of operation. Walt Disney World in Florida opened sixteen years later and annually attracts over 52 million guests each year.

> "When you believe in a thing, believe in it all the way, implicitly and unquestionably."
>
> —Walt Disney

The Fabric of Who We Are

Values are standards and behaviors that we deem important in life. When your values align with your actions, your authentic light shines. When they do not, life can seem harsh and meaningless. Walt Disney placed a high value on family, and his goal was to create a world in which families could experience the simple joys in life. That focus determined his priorities and he mapped out his goals accordingly.

Values are important to the life mapping process because scientific research resoundingly supports connecting our goals to our respective underlying values. They represent what's most important to us; therefore, we usually have a strong, sturdy sense of self wrapped up in their meaning. We'll fight to protect our values.

Values create a link from who we are fundamentally to "what's up" for us this year and currently deserving of our attention. It makes sense then that our goals should be prioritized and checked to ensure they support our core values.

Values are similar to beliefs in that they are largely shaped by our environments and how we grew up. The values demonstrated by our parents and closest family members often become our own. In addition, our individual life-defining experiences shape the specific meaning we attach to the words we choose to represent our values. For example, freedom and what it means to one person will likely be defined very differently by another. As Dr. Markman explained, since these concepts are "abstract instead of concrete, we cannot touch and feel our values in a tangible sense."

Connecting with our core values helps us understand where we should specifically focus our time and attention. Markman suggests that our fundamental beliefs and principles really won't change much over time; on the other hand, it is quite possible for our values to shift over the course of a year and highly probable they'll shift as we age. An example would be if a family member is suddenly diagnosed with a terminal illness, aging parents suddenly need more of our time, or you (or your significant other) lose your job. Family, connection, or career may instantly become the leading value for the current year. Also, as we get older, things that were once a priority, like career, won't be as important when we retire. Our priorities will change.

The reason it's important to review our values, at least annually, is because they are the gas powering the motor in everything we do. When we're in touch and living a life aligned with what's most important to us, we are more motivated, inspired, and satisfied. Focusing on goals that serve our values results in meeting our own needs, and this is an expression of self-love and self-care. When we're not directing our goals toward our values, we may feel unhappy, lost, frustrated, and unmotivated. Values drive the major decisions we make regarding family, career, finances, intimate relationships, physical and spiritual health, and personal aspirations.

Like everything we're learning in *Live Your Gift,* regular review and intentional practice of these concepts is vitally important. Gregory Maio gives a good example in his post about understanding human values. If the environment is a core value and a person has been reviewing those values, the next time they have a handful of papers to throw away, they'll be much more likely to toss it in the recycling bin. He says, "The time spent thinking about protection of the environment acts as a reminder that this value is important, which makes people mindful of it during their next opportunity to act accordingly." Even though these concepts may exist within us, specifically identifying them makes them even more powerful.

Beliefs answer the "*WHY* are we here?" question. Principles answer the "*HOW* do we want to show up in the world?" question. Values provide the answer to "*WHAT* feelings do we want to experience more of because we find them satisfying?"

Here's *Merriam-Webster's* definition of "value":

> **Value:** Relative worth, utility, or importance. Intrinsically valuable or desirable.

Values are the underlying motivators for springing out of bed in the morning versus hitting the snooze button. Values are typically one word and they represent the feelings, emotions, and priorities we want to experience more of as we move through our year.

Our Values List boils down to three to five separate words that capture the essence of our definition of a fulfilling year. Values Lists are personal, and there is no right or wrong list or order of priority. Focusing our daily, weekly, monthly, and yearlong activities on goals that support our core values produces the most ideal outcome. We'll select one value as our leading value, which serves as a guide for the many decisions we will make in the year ahead. Our leading value represents the one thing, above all else, that we'd like to illuminate and make sure we dedicate time toward. I envision the leading value as the high beams and the other values as the headlights, fog lights, and blinkers on our car. One big value illuminating the road ahead and all the others guiding us safely to our destination.

Self-Awareness

I've heard a lot of people say, "It's all about compromise." Whether it's an intimate relationship, kids, best friend, or boss, compromise is one thing, but turning our back on our values altogether is another. How do we know the difference? One will leave us feeling like we found positive or fair middle ground. The other will leave us feeling violated. Compromise is give and take; easy come, easy go; or finding gray in the midst of black-and-white thinking. If we give in a little more this time and the scale tips slightly away from us, we know next time it will tip back in our direction.

Turning our back on our values is like turning around and walking away from ourselves. Actually, to say we're abandoning ourselves is more accurate. If we tune in to our bodies, we'll feel it; we won't physically feel right; it's icky. Our body and mind react to being out of integrity. We call this intuitive knowing our "gut," or we say we can *feel* it at our "core" and we just *know* that something is off.

In his article "Cognitive Dissonance," Saul McLeod revealed that having internal conflict between what we know is right and taking action in opposition to those beliefs results in cognitive dissonance. Cognitive dissonance, in this instance, means having a thought that is in direct opposition to our beliefs or values. An example of this would be really caring about your best friend, but recently she's smoking marijuana (and not for medical reasons) and it's impacting her ability to be present with you when you're together. You do not believe in using drugs, legal or not. As a result, your body's response is an increase in cortisol levels, which is triggered by the fight-or-flight phenomenon and leaves you feeling anxious or uncomfortable.

This is a slippery slope because when we try to justify or minimize those opposing beliefs to make ourselves feel better about consciously deciding to stay friends, it creates a prolonged stress on the body. The discord never really goes away, even though we try to justify our decisions. Prolonged dissonance and cortisol flooding produce stress. We all know stress takes its toll on the physical body, resulting in symptoms like anxiety, lower immune function, depression, elevated blood pressure, and many other ailments. As we become aware of what we believe and the standards we want to live by, we learn to make better decisions in support of our overall physical, emotional, and mental health.

One of the many benefits of having a clear list of values is to become that much more attuned to how we need to prioritize our time. In addition, if we do start to notice our gut churning, we'll know where to turn to uncover the answer to why. Recently, I experienced a perfect example of this. One of my friends was hosting a full-day styling event in mid-March. In my excitement to support her, and because I love learning and can always use styling tips, I jumped at the chance to sign up. There were only thirty spots, so I quickly decided "I'm in!"

In my haste, I didn't stop to evaluate my month and the goals I set for myself. Within twenty-four hours of receiving my confirmation, I knew I had made a mistake. Not because I didn't really want to go, but because I was out of alignment. I set a goal months ago that I wanted to pass the manuscript to the copy editor by March 31. I was working within a tight window. How did I know I made a mistake?

As soon as the thought came to mind asking, "Dana, what are you doing? Do you think you will be done with the book? Can you justify going to the event? Do you think you will have the extra time and be able to be present and enjoy being there? Or is it more important to make your deadline and be in alignment with your goal?"

Integrity is one of my core values; so is well-being. I wouldn't have felt good being at the event if I wasn't done with the book. I'd be kicking myself mentally for misusing my time and being out of integrity with myself if I didn't hit my deadline, and the stress wouldn't contribute to my well-being. In addition to being out of alignment with my values, I was out of sync with my principle that says, "I will only make commitments I can keep," and in that case, I would be out of line with my belief that I have an ability to make a positive impact in other people's lives. So what did I do? I waited a few weeks to see what kind of progress I was making on the book. Then, when the event was a week out and I knew I'd need the time to work on the book, I contacted my friend. I was truthful with my friend about the predicament I found myself in. I didn't ask for a refund (this was my error, not hers) and I suggested offering my seat (with her blessing, of course) to a good friend who I knew would love to be there but couldn't afford the ticket. She was in total support of my suggestion and completely understood. With the weight off my shoulders, I took a deep breath and knew I'd made the right decision.

Our values help supply the vision for where we want to go. It's now time to complete the values exercise, so let's get started.

What are the most important things to you at this point in your life? There are a multitude of core value exercises, and I will provide two of them for you. Completing both may help you feel highly confident in your selections.

This first list of questions I borrowed from IQ Matrix owner Adam Sicinski. He lives in Melbourne, Australia, and has vast knowledge of the importance of values. I encourage you to check out his website for the tools and information he has to offer: www.iqmatrix.com.

On a piece of paper or in the *Live Your Gift Companion Guide*, answer the following questions to help identify what bubbles to the surface regarding your priorities. These questions are compelling, as they begin with a long-term view and then progressively force you to take a shorter-term view of your life and priorities. Your values will, of course, probably be very different with six years to live compared with having only six minutes to live. The difference, however, isn't important. What's important here is that you notice how your priorities change, moving from a span of years to minutes.

Keep your answers to single words to encapsulate your priorities.

- What would I do if I only had six years to live?
- What would I do if I only had six months to live?
- What would I do if I only had six weeks to live?
- What would I do if I only had six days to live?
- What would I do if I only had six hours to live?
- What would I do if I only had six minutes to live?

Look through what you have written and circle the five words that are the driving force behind your answers. Number your values in order of priority. Select your number one leading value and write that word in the Leading Value box. Then list the other words in order of priority below it.

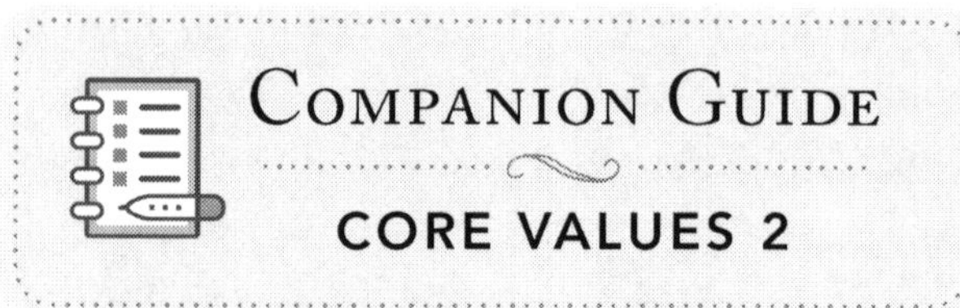

Follow the steps below to identify your core values.

Note that you can visit www.lifemappinginstitute.com/resources to download the worksheet.

1. Circle each word from the list on page 62 that resonates with you. Don't overthink your selections. As you read through the list, trust your instincts, but circle only the words you feel genuinely align with the priorities you have for your life. If you find there's a word that's important, yet you are not currently living your life with that word in the forefront, circle it anyway, especially if you feel it's optimal. You should have approximately 15–20 words circled that resonate with you.
2. On a piece of paper or in the *Companion Guide*, rewrite the words you circled and group the words together that you think have similar meaning. For example: *fitness*, *balance*, and *vitality* may all be words you associate with your health and feeling good. Go ahead and group these words together.

3. Now go back through the words and choose a word or two within each group that you feel most connected to and circle it. You may find that one word more accurately gives meaning to a few things that are important to you. For example: *success*, *achievement*, *accomplishment*, and *leadership* may all be in the same group. Ultimately, you may decide the word *achievement* really means you succeeded and accomplished what you set out to do, so you only need that word. *Leadership* may still be an important value and you may realize it means something completely different than what *achievement* means. In that case, you would keep the word *achievement* and the word *leadership*.
4. Whittle your list to your top three to five words overall.
5. Number your values in order of priority. Select your number one leading value and write that word in the Leading Value box. Then list the other words in order of priority below it.
6. Write a sentence next to each word and reaffirm why the value is important to you
7. Reflect on your life right now. Are you living in alignment with these words? If not, what would you need to do to feel more in alignment with your core values? Make a mental note and put a star next to any values you would like to reengage with. We'll check in with this list once you choose your priority goals.

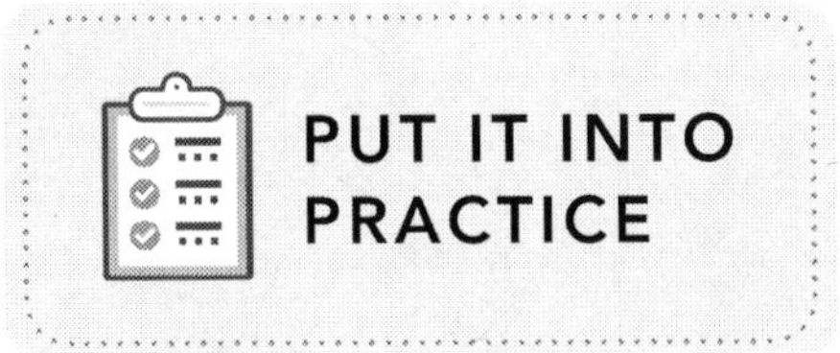

VALUES EXERCISE

Acceptance	Common sense	Enlightenment	Health	Nurture	Self-worth
Accomplishment	Communication	Entertainment	Honesty	Observation	Sensuality
Accountability	Community	Enthusiasm	Honor	Openness	Serenity
Accuracy	Compassion	Environment	Hope	Optimism	Service
Achievement	Competence	Ethics	Humility	Order	Sharing
Acknowledgment	Connection	Excellence	Humor	Organization	Significance
Acquisition	Consciousness	Experience	Independence	Originality	Silence
Adventure	Consideration	Experimental	Individuality	Passion	Simplicity
Alertness	Contentment	Expertise	Influence	Peace	Sincerity
Alignment	Contribution	Exploration	Inner peace	Performance	Skillfulness
Altruism	Cooperation	Expressive	Innovation	Persistence	Smart
Ambition	Courage	Facilitate	Inquisitive	Personal development	Solitude
Amusement	Courageous	Fairness	Insightful	Personal growth	Spirituality
Assertiveness	Creative	Faith	Inspiration	Play	Spontaneous
Assistance	Daring	Fame	Inspire	Popularity	Stability
Attentive	Decisiveness	Family	Integrity	Professionalism	Status
Authenticity	Dedication	Feeling good	Intelligence	Proficiency	Strength
Authority	Delightful	Fidelity	Intensity	Provider	Structure
Balance	Dependability	Fitness	Intuitive	Realistic	Success
Beauty	Determination	Focus	Inventiveness	Recreation	Superiority
Being present	Devotion	Foresight	Kindness	Reflection	Sustainability
Bliss	Dignity	Fortitude	Laughter	Relatedness	Teaching
Boldness	Direct	Freedom	Lawful	Relationships	Teamwork
Bravery	Discipline	Friendship	Leadership	Relaxation	Thankful
Calm	Distinguished	Fun	Learning	Reliability	Tolerance
Candor	Diversity	Generosity	Logic	Religion	Trust
Capable	Drive	Genius	Love	Reputation	Trustworthiness
Careful	Economic security	Giving	Loyalty	Respect	Truthfulness
Certainty	Education	Grace	Magnificence	Responsibility	Understanding
Challenged	Effectiveness	Gratitude	Mastery	Results	Unity
Charity	Elegance	Greatness	Maturity	Risk	Vision
Citizenship	Emotional well-being	Growth	Meaningful work	Safety	Wealth
Cleanliness	Empathy	Guidance	Merriment	Security	Well-being
Coach	Empowerment	Happiness	Moderation	Self-awareness	Wellness
Comfort	Encouragement	Hard work	Nature	Selfless	Wholeness
Commitment	Enjoyment	Harmony	Nobility	Self-reliance	Wisdom

Optimal Me

Optimal Me is a list of seven to ten daily, weekly, or bimonthly habits that provide a snapshot for how you operate in the world at optimal capacity. It's a quick weekly check-in to gauge your emotional, physical, spiritual, and intellectual health. I was introduced to the idea fourteen years ago as a participant in a three-year program through the Center for Authentic Leadership. The idea is to recognize those things we do regularly as a matter of habit. We do these things because they support who we are, what makes us feel good, and how we like to show up in our world when life is humming along like a well-oiled machine.

Here's my list to give you an idea:

OPTIMAL ME

Make My Bed Daily	Eating 85–90% Clean During the Week	Write Gratitudes Daily
Work Out with My Trainer 3x per Week	Return All Business Calls & Email Within 24 Hours	Dinner with the Kids at the Table 3–4x per Week
Clean Car Inside and Out Every Week–10 Days	Time with Boys: Listening, Affection, Appreciation	Checkbook Up to Date Every 10–14 Days
Dishes in the Dishwasher at Night	House Picked Up	Sleep 7+ hours

On occasion, I notice I haven't made my bed for several days. Since it's something I normally do, and I like how I feel walking into my bedroom seeing a well-made bed, I start to get curious with myself about why I left my bed messy. Sometimes I tell myself I simply don't feel like it and move along with what I'm doing by giving myself a hall pass. However, if a few days later I'm still not making my bed and my car is looking rather dirty because I haven't washed it in a few weeks, then I know something's up. Two weeks is a long time in rainy Washington with boys, dirty cleats, and the possibility that clients may need to jump in my car at a moment's notice. If later that same day I return home to see shoes, couch pillows, and blankets tossed about, it's definitely a clue I need to check in with myself!

Simply having awareness of my normal MO (modus operandi)/ OM (optimal me) means I have a defined set of activities I'm usually attentive to. When my actions are considerably outside the norm, I have an awareness and tool in place to help me re-center. The last time this happened was not long after my oldest son's dad passed away. I felt sad and unmotivated, and I wasn't ready to interact with the outside world. I didn't stay in that mental state for too long, but acknowledging that's where I was, I gave myself permission to "be" in the grief and loss.

I believe there are times when the healthiest, loving action we can take toward ourselves is letting go of structure so we can genuinely feel our feelings and just "be." Of course, if I'm feeling off-center for more than a few weeks, I jump on the phone and make an appointment with my therapist. We need to take responsibility for all aspects of our health. We cannot wait and live in a fantasy that someone will rescue us. I think everyone benefits by knowing how they define their typical, healthy task list.

It's time to define the optimal you.

> "The moment you take responsibility for everything in your life is the moment you can change anything in your life."
>
> —Hal Elrod

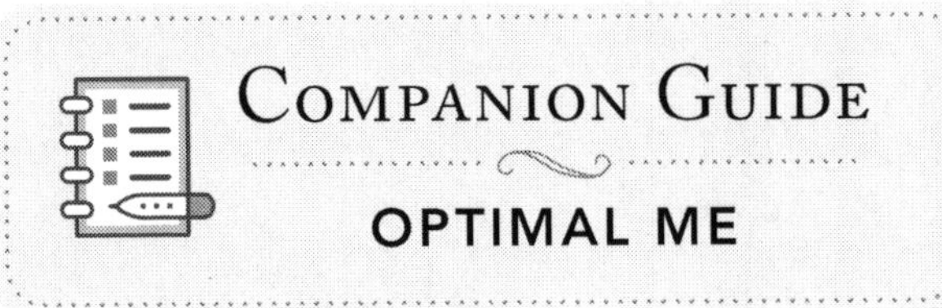

On a piece of paper or in your *Live Your Gift Companion Guide*, answer the following question:

What are the activities you normally perform on a daily, weekly, or bimonthly basis?

If you're not doing these things, you would know something's distracting you and you're likely off track. Think of the tasks you are usually responsible for and how you typically take care of yourself and your home.

Examples:

- Laundry
- Dishes
- Housework
- Automobiles
- Exercise
- Eating
- Grocery shopping
- Finances
- Landscaping and gardening
- Family and friends
- Beauty (showering, brushing your teeth, shaving, putting on makeup, doing your hair)
- Physical health

Pure Joy

Pure joy represents all the things we love to do, experience, and appreciate without expectation of anyone giving back to us or for financial compensation. It's beauty we admire, sights that take our breath away, moments when time stands still, and participation in activities we emphatically love.

Writing about pure joy brings a smile to my face. It's such a simple concept and yet, we can all use so many more joyful moments in our lives. Jan Smith, founder of the Center for Authentic Leadership, is the wonderful teacher and wise woman who opened my eyes and brought awareness to moments that fill my heart with effortless joy. You deserve to recognize these times as well. Like some of our gifts, these appreciations may in part be influenced by those we love. But no matter where they come from, they're personally unique to your world. When we see, taste, smell, touch, or feel these joyful moments, they sing a melodious song to our soul and tie a beautiful ribbon around our experience of life. Joy is often unpredictable, like when Mother Nature blesses us with a watercolor sunset.

Incredible sunsets take my breath away. I'm the sunset chaser in my family; I'll go the distance to get closer. I want to see the tapestry unfold and soak in the beauty of nature's magic. The boys know this about me now, so they go along with my curiosity and enjoy them right along with me. I hope long after I'm flying with the angels, they'll be chasing those painted skies with their kids, too.

Joy emits powerful emotions. The sensation is sometimes so strong it captures the emotional essence of the experience and imprints the memory on our soul for a lifetime. We never know when these moments may occur but what a blessing when they do.

By creating a list of our passions, we raise our awareness for how we define pure joy. This, in turn, allows us to set more time aside to enjoy what makes us happy. Cherishing and experiencing simple pleasures adds to our overall experience and enjoyment in life.

When we feel overwhelmed, frazzled, stressed, anxious, and upset and need a pick-me-up or just want to feel more goodness more often, we can reground ourselves by choosing to do something we love. In counseling, it's referred to as distress tolerance. When we're in distress or feeling emotions that put us in our "back seat," we can take a break by doing an activity on our list.

> "The light of everlasting life lit up in the soul."
>
> —*Book of Mormon*

Here's a sample of the items on my Pure Joy List:

SIGHT	SMELL	TASTE	TOUCH	SOUND
Sunsets	Baked pastries	Ice cream	Baking	Music on surround sound
Manicured landscaping & flowers	Blooming flowers	Filet mignon and baked potatoes	Sewing	Boys playing piano
Lake water	Spring potpourri	Fresh warm bread and butter	Walking by the lake	Books on Audible
Pictures of the boys	Burberry perfume	Warm apple pie à la mode	Journaling	Live music

It is time to think about what brings you fulfillment and joy without any expectation or conditional outcome. You should enjoy these things because you love and appreciate their beauty and/or how they make you feel, not for money, reward, or recognition.

In your *Live Your Gift Companion Guide* or on a piece of paper, create your Pure Joy List.

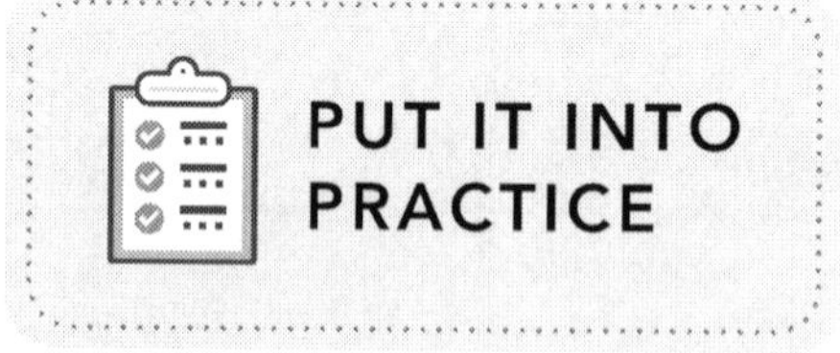

CHAPTER FIVE

Your Goals

> "Do something today your future self will thank you for."
>
> —Sean Patrick Flanery

Living Their Gift

James's kindergarten teacher suspected he had ADHD. While he tested one grade level ahead of his peers, he was indeed diagnosed with the condition. He didn't begin to run into issues until tenth grade. He excelled in math, foreign languages, and piano but had a very difficult time concentrating on reading. When it came to writing essays or reports, it was pure torture. Here he was, a straight-A student who suddenly couldn't manage to type a single paragraph in three hours. His grades began to nose-dive.

Upon transferring from private to public school, things went from bad to worse academically. He continued to pull an easy A in some subjects, but in others he struggled terribly. James was disappointed in himself for letting his grades slide. He knew it meant he wouldn't have as many choices for college. He was accepted to Washington State University, but he also considered going into the military. His ambitious dream of becoming a Navy SEAL was quickly dashed when he was told the U.S. military wouldn't accept anyone who had a history of asthma, which he did.

James set off with lofty goals of earning straight A's at school. He joined a fraternity, lived in a dorm, and was lifting weights religiously. But by midterms he was struggling. He came home for a weekend visit in mid-October and his normal sparkle and zest for life weren't there. He was partying at college with his frat brothers, which wasn't ever his thing in high school, skipping workouts, getting into fights, and struggling to get to class. He decided to withdraw right before Thanksgiving break.

Reluctantly, he enrolled in the local community college and said he would pursue a job at a bank. When he landed a full-time position at Key Bank as a teller, he quickly excelled there, hitting his sales goals, receiving numerous awards, bonuses, promotions, and offers to attend special advanced trainings. He worked diligently at school, earning quarterly Dean's List recognition, enlisting a good friend to become his weekly accountability partner, and making his plans for his next move

after he earned his associate's degree.

Then his father, Pat, had complications following hip surgery. As his father's primary health care power of attorney, James had to decide if the doctors should intubate him. He was just twenty years old at the time. He told the doctors not to intubate, as he knew those were his dad's wishes. Pat passed away with James by his side.

You do not know James. He is not a celebrity or activist or world-class athlete. But he is a rock star—to me. He is my son. I clearly remember the bravery, strength, and courage James displayed that night his father passed. After the pain of losing his dad, with much of the summer spent processing what had happened, James decided he would stop working and go to school full time. He has since taken twenty credits for the past four quarters and is on track to graduate in the spring of 2019 from the University of Washington Foster School of Business with a 3.8 GPA.

James exemplifies what it means to get back up after being knocked down. He experienced learning challenges in high school and had to come to terms with his ADHD. He had a failed attempt at Washington State University, only to fight his way into the UW Foster School of Business, where he's excelling with honors. He endured the staggering loss of his dad, whom he loved with all his heart. His resilience and perseverance will always be strengths to fall back on when life knocks him down. James is keeping his sights locked on working in investment banking. No doubt, he is well on his way to living his gift!

> "Success isn't something that just happens. You've got to be willing to do what it takes, day in and day out, even when you can't see the results yet."
>
> —James Corbett

In the Driver's Seat

Goals change, sometimes by our own design and sometimes by external forces that we cannot control. But to successfully chart our course, to map out our lives, we must have goals because they are our desired destinations. They are the visions we create because we believe they are worthy of our attention and effort.

The lists we developed in the Beliefs, Principles, and Values chapters are the foundation upon which we will build our goals. We should not have a goal that conflicts with anything on our lists. Some people say they don't have any goals. What they mean is that they can't see a way of achieving their dreams. Turning a dream into a goal requires planning, vision, and willingness to follow through.

People who focus on the future have an amazing opportunity to manifest their desires. If our thoughts are positive, we will attract positive to us. We all know that as the Law of Attraction. I love what Larry Kendall, motivational speaker and author of the sales mastery book *Ninja Selling*, had to say during the seminar I attended in 2011. Larry's speaking style is grounded, caring, genuine, and nurturing in a fatherly way. As he was building us up to imagine amazing things for ourselves, he said confidently, "What you focus on expands." He went on to explain that if we focus on our future, then we'll create the future we seek. Our internal, subconscious, goal-seeking mechanism will begin working to make our vision materialize. We must still do the work, but now it's as if we have a campaign manager on our team.

If you're reading this book, you probably don't need to be convinced that goal setting puts you in the driver's seat of your life. Planning and envisioning future possibilities points us in a positive direction so that we live with intention. Decades of research affirm the positive effects of setting goals and aiming for achievement, when done in the right context. Researchers Locke and Latham are experts in the goal-setting theory of motivation. Their conclusions support the following recommendations:

1. Set challenging goals, but you must believe they are attainable.
2. Be engaged and have willingness to follow through.
3. Be as specific as possible.
4. Tie your goals to expected performance outcomes.
5. Be accountable to someone who will provide input on your progress.
6. Use target dates to stay on track.

Not only do we experience positive outcomes by achieving our goals, but the act of setting goals, hearing feedback along the way, and believing we're capable of attaining our goals elevates our sense of well-being. What can we take away from this research? One, setting goals produces positive results. Two, you must believe you are capable of completing the task or learning the new skills necessary to finish the task. If you don't believe it's possible, it won't be a worthy goal.

If the goal is too big or overwhelming, cut it into bite-size pieces. Dr. Srini Pillay, author of *Tinker Dabble Doodle Try*, suggests reframing the goal into one that feels more manageable. For example: Let's say you currently make $50,000 per year in sales and you'd really love to earn $100,000 per year. But the truth is it was challenging to attain $50,000 and it still seems like a massive stretch to jump to $100,000. It's better to start with a number you do believe is within your reach. Ask yourself if you think an increase of $10,000 or $20,000 is more attainable. Once you find a number that's believable in your gut, go with it and set that as your new benchmark. Once you knock that one down, you'll be ready to jump to the next number.

Goals can always be adjusted up or down to increase the likelihood for success. This isn't meant to let you off the hook from setting a challenging goal; on the contrary, you're taking the time up front to be in complete integrity with yourself so that you will. There's no point in setting yourself up for failure by starting with something that seems beyond your reach. Remember, it's the right combination of commitment, specificity, accountability, and a belief you can succeed that makes the goal achievable.

The underlying theme behind goal setting is taking control and then maintaining control of your life. Determine what *you* want; don't let others limit you with their expectations. Ask yourself what you would be doing with your life if success were guaranteed.

Perceived Limitations?

When people think about goals, they usually come face-to-face with their perceived limitations. Instead of thinking about your limitations, the potential problems, or the negative results that might occur, think about the rewards to be gained by reaching each new goal. The gains waiting for us far outweigh the risks involved. Don't let the problems keep you from seeing the possibilities. We will address silent threats to our success and how to prepare safe detours around them in the next chapter, but for now, allow yourself to dream without limitation.

One man, British runner Roger Bannister, saw the possibility of breaking the four-minute mile barrier. It had never been done before, but he believed it was possible. Once he determined he was going to be the one to accomplish the feat, he hired a coach and recruited a few other runners to train with him. Training was incredibly challenging and at times he wanted to throw in the towel. One of Bannister's track mates, Chris Chataway, recalls the coach, Franz Stampfl, encouraging them to persevere by saying, "If you could get a world record, it would be as good as painting the *Mona Lisa*; your place in world history would be secured."

Tony Federico, vice president of marketing for Naturalforce.com, wrote a short story called "Achieving the Impossible" about Bannister's race at Oxford on May 6, 1954:

"Fighting against otherworldly fatigue, Bannister commanded his legs to move. He knew that this could be his last opportunity to do the impossible—to break the four-minute mile, and to secure his place in the history books. A final kick and he was through the tape, and within a few steps, he collapsed into the arms of an official . . .

"Finally, the announcer's voice rang out: 'Event 9. One Mile.' The announcer paused for effect before continuing. 'First: R. G. Bannister with a time which is a Ground Record, a British Record, a British All-Comer's Record, a European Record, a British Empire Record, and a World Record of three . . .' The crowd exploded into cheering before the announcer could finish . . . '3:59.4.'"

Roger believed it was possible and it was! He lived a long life and passed away on March 3, 2018, at the age of 88. He tore down the barrier and in his lifetime saw another 1,300 runners break the four-minute mile. Time continues to show us that what once seemed inconceivable is absolutely achievable. The current world record time for the one mile is held by Hicham El Guerrouj from Morocco: 3:43.13. Almost 17 seconds less than Bannister's record! Incredible!

How close have you come to achieving your potential? What goals will test your perceived limits and bring your achievements closer to your potential? Don't be afraid to explore new horizons. Overcome the temptation to maintain the status quo; seek the adventure and happiness that awaits you along the path. Simply writing down your goals will not guarantee success. Following that with the action steps that will be developed in the next several chapters will put the odds overwhelmingly in your favor.

Seeking Balance

The act of deciding on our goals is a very important step. A big portion of our lives becomes the goals we actively pursue. As James Allen, author of *As a Man Thinketh*, says, "Until thought is linked with purpose there is no intelligent accomplishment. With most people the bark of thought is allowed to drift upon the ocean of life. . . . We need to conceive of a legitimate purpose in our heart and set out to accomplish it."

One obstacle we will face along the way is this idea of balance. Visualize a BOSU balance trainer. Have you ever tried standing on one? A BOSU is a piece of exercise equipment that looks like half of a big, thick blown-up rubber exercise ball. It's inflated on one side and has a flat, hard-plastic surface on the other. Well, if you've ever attempted standing and balancing on one, you know it's not easy. You start by turning it over so the round, inflated rubber side is down. Then, very carefully, you step one foot on as it teeters right over to the weight of your foot, while gracefully, stepping your other foot onto the opposite side that's now tilted high up in the air. I'm typically hanging onto something stable, like a wall, until I have both of my feet on, and even that's a challenge.

You can probably guess where I'm going with this. Finding perfect balance in life is more difficult than it sounds. We've all been told that balance is ideal, and most of us probably buy into this idea, but realistically, life is usually in a state of flux. If we're hanging out on the BOSU with our legs shaking, there's going to be a little wobbling, and that's OK. We're still on the ball; it's how we know we're working and in the "game." Obviously, it stands to reason that if we completely lift one foot without supporting ourselves by moving our other foot closer to center, we're going to lose balance and fall off the BOSU. It's OK; that's going to happen.

The point is to keep an eye on how you're balancing all aspects of your life. I call the various categories of my life "pillars." Yes, just like pillars architects design to support large structures. The more intentional we are about allocating time between our pillars, the more centered we'll feel.

If you're working longer and are more focused on your career, saving the rest of the daytime hours for family but neglecting diet and exercise, you can count on your pants feeling tighter in a few weeks. When you begin to establish goals in different areas of your life, think about limits that truly express your idea of "enough." How much income is enough? When is a house big enough? Do you need to own a vacation home or is renting enough? How many pairs of shoes do you really need?

During my twenty-three years in the real estate industry, I have learned a lot from the market's highs and lows. A market on the rise generates a lot of income and, likewise, the fall can be devastating. Life is also one big cycle. When we are young, under thirty, we think we are going to live forever; we spend all that we earn and then some and believe we will have more than enough time to plan for retirement. Between the ages of thirty and fifty, we shift to the accumulation stage. We buy houses, fancy cars, art, nice furniture, and designer clothes. Then, between fifty and sixty-five, when the children are grown and have moved out, we begin wondering, "What are we going to do with all this stuff?" Finally, sometime in our seventies, we figure out how we're going to give it all away. If we could start the next cycle with a better understanding of what is truly important to us, we would come to the later stages better prepared. Our preparation will allow us to understand that what we have is not nearly as important as who we become.

In creating your own support pillars, you'll decide on the names for each. The specific names are not as important as adequately covering all the areas you consider important. For example, one person may like to use the term "Career" to cover the work aspects of their life, while another who may not be working, may use "School" or "Personal Development." Naming your pillars is up to you; choose titles you like. I suggest choosing four to six pillars. I find it easier to track my goals this way, but if you prefer eight, please do what works for you. My life map has six pillars: Family, Career, Spiritual, Financial Security, Physical, and Creature Comforts. Here's a generous selection of possible titles; feel free to add your own:

GOAL PILLARS

Spiritual	Career	Family	Emotional
Finances	Friends	Health	Personal Growth
Love	Romance	Recreation	Professional
Fun	Business	Relationships	Social
Environmental	Adventure	Studies	Contribution
Fitness	Excitement	Intellectual	School
Creativity	Travel	Religion	Creature Comforts

My World of Wellness

My World of Wellness Wheel shows the relationship of my six goal pillars to my personal well-being. The optimal goal of personal well-being is that each one of us be in the center of our wheel. If your personal spirit is weak or a last priority, you will not be living your healthiest life. Health, vitality, and balance come from constantly paying attention to making yourself a priority as you move out to focus on the other important aspects of your life.

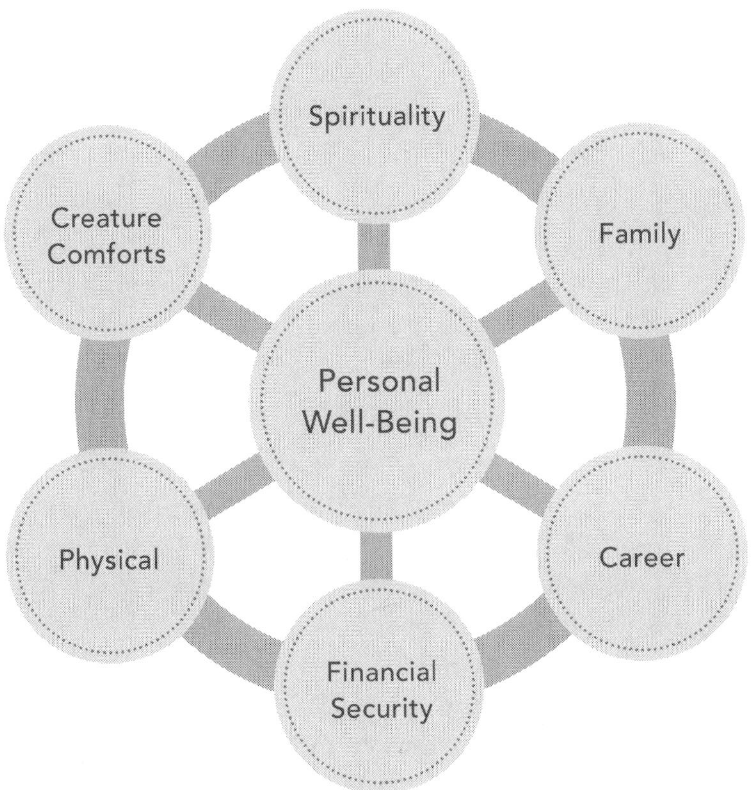

Write It Down

You may have heard the old saying "The journey of a thousand miles begins with a single step." It is much easier to blaze a new trail when you have a guide leading the way. Materializing your goals begins when you commit them to writing. It is one thing to say you have goal; it is quite another to act. Are you ready to take the first step? Let's go!

In the next exercise, we are going to allow our minds and creativity to flow. I call this worksheet the 100s List. The object is to ask yourself over and over, "What do I want?" I'm challenging you to complete the form in its entirety! Some people become blocked after they have ten or fifteen things written down. I want you to think bigger and broader, and play with this like a game. It doesn't mean you are greedy if you fill up your worksheet with creature comforts. This activity is an opportunity to unload all the great ideas we carry around in our heads—all the goals we'd love to accomplish, things we need to do, people we'd like to help, items we need to buy or would like to buy, and things we'd like to experience, learn, and give.

You can use the following prompts to help you along. First, answer this question for each of your pillars:

- What do I want in this area of my life? For example: What do I want to accomplish with my family?

Here are some additional prompts to consider:

- What is your ideal vision of the person you want to become?
- How do you want to be remembered?
- If failure weren't an option, what would you love to be doing?
- If finances were plentiful, what would you do?
- Is there a skill you'd like to learn?

- Think through your typical day. Are there things you tolerate but need to repair?
- Are there things you could use to make your life easier that you don't currently have?
- Do you need to rid yourself of certain things? What do you need to declutter?
- Can't get focused? Then write down what you need to do to get organized.
- Think about your significant other, kids, family, and friends. Are there things you would like to do with them? For them?
- Do you have work to do on your emotional health?
- Do you have work to do on your spiritual health?
- How's your physical health?
- Do you have bills to pay off?
- Do you have savings?
- If you knew you were going to die in a year, what would you want to do?

A few important notes. The 100s List isn't time bound. If you have a goal you think you may want to accomplish but it's likely ten years out, write it down. If there's something on your mind, like picking up the dry-cleaning this week, write it down. This list should include goals you believe are achievable. You may not know *how* you will get there, but you have a belief *you will*. Write it all down and have fun! In another chapter, we'll be much more specific about making our prioritized goals time bound as well as creating a plan to accomplish them. You should be able to complete this list within thirty minutes.

Here's a little more food for thought, as well as examples of goals from past workshop participants.

Family

Your vision might include the kind of spouse, parent, sibling, or child you want to become. How would you like to act in each of these relationships? What kinds of things would you enjoy doing?

Sample Family Goals

1. Check in with my spouse daily.
2. Teach the kids the positive lessons my parents taught me.
3. Work to be a good mom by taking parenting classes every year.
4. Learn our family tree.
5. Complete Ancestry DNA test.
6. Show love and affection to my kids daily.
7. Enjoy one family activity every week.
8. Write Grandma and Grandpa a letter once a month.
9. Check in with Mom and Dad weekly to see if they need my help.
10. Cook once a week for tent city homeless camp.

Spiritual

Your vision might include any or many of the following: developing your relationship with God or another Higher Power, living in harmony with nature, learning to understand yourself through meditation, connecting with universal consciousness, understanding your subconscious, or taking walks along the lake. This is not a complete list; it is intended to spark your imagination.

Sample Spiritual Goals

1. Attend one or two yoga classes per week.
2. Read four nonfiction books this year.

3. Write down my gratitude in a journal every day.
4. Watch a personal-growth video once a week.
5. Take three hikes this summer.
6. Attend two charity auctions this year.
7. Volunteer to supply food for high school events.
8. Attend three new churches in the next three months.
9. Take walks along the lake twice a week.
10. Discuss God with my children and help them develop their own personal understanding of spirituality.

Physical

Your vision might include discovering a new exercise class, strength training, losing weight, developing lifestyle habits that promote longevity, getting adequate sleep, practicing intermittent fasting, avoiding tobacco, or moderating or abstaining from alcohol.

Sample Physical Goals

1. Maintain my ideal weight of 185 pounds.
2. Exercise three times a week.
3. Strength-train at least three days a week.
4. Drink eight glasses of water daily.
5. Eliminate smoking from my life.
6. Abstain from alcohol this year.
7. Take a self-defense class within the next six months.
8. Eliminate pork from my diet.
9. Take a hike into the Enchantments this summer.
10. Do 100 push-ups, sit-ups, and kick-outs per day.

Professional/Personal

You will spend more time in your vocation than in any other activity you will participate in, except sleeping. Hopefully, you're in a career you love! If you're not, there's no time like the present to plan a transition. Ask yourself: If we lived in a world without money, what would you be doing? Your vision for your career or personal growth may include raising your children, learning to cook, travel, leading work teams, or involvement with politics, civil organizations, or charities.

Sample Professional/Personal Goals

1. Find a career that involves tasks that I love doing before I graduate.
2. Spend one hour a week updating my database.
3. Learn about a new culture every year.
4. Volunteer weekly at a local hospital while I'm in nursing school.
5. Listen to my co-workers' ideas.
6. Invest $1,000 in a welding class.
7. Sign up for a cooking class on making sauces.
8. Take a GMAT preparation class this year.
9. Work monthly on increasing my performance at work.
10. Work daily on expressing my opinion.

Speaking of career, there is a little book called *The Animal School* by George H. Reavis that tells the story of a school attended by different kinds of animals. The school decided to test the animals in a variety of areas. One particular duck, an excellent swimmer and flier, turned out to be a very poor runner, so in their infinite wisdom, the school officials decided that the duck could no longer swim or fly until he improved his running. Soon he became an average runner, but for some unexplained reason, he also became only an average swimmer and flier.

Don't let anyone influence you into giving up skills that come naturally and that you enjoy! Likewise, if being the household handyperson isn't your thing, find someone you can hire to do it for you. Life is too short trying to be someone or something you're not! One of my coaches, Jessica Butts, says, "Be unapologetically who you are!" I love that saying because it's a great reminder to embrace our natural skills, abilities, and passions without exception. It's a great way to own who we are, have belief and confidence in ourselves, and never apologize because we may not know how to do something. We don't owe anyone an explanation for what makes us happy or how we choose to spend our time.

In certain pursuits, we may need additional education. If there's a skill you need to acquire to advance professionally, then make that a goal! Always allow your natural creativity and curiosity to work for you.

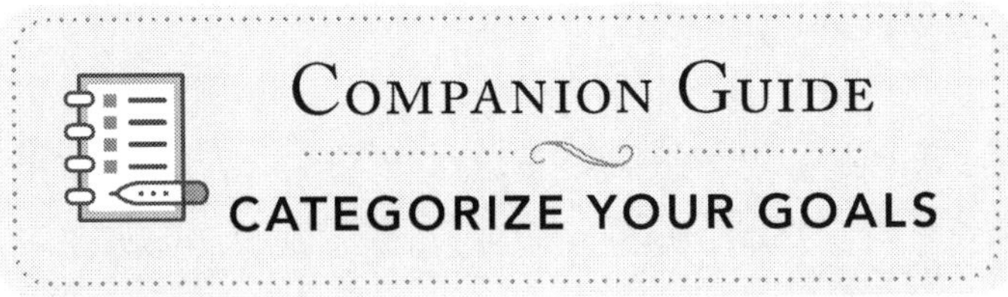

Now that you have completed your 100s List, you'll want to put them into the appropriate categories, or pillars, that correspond with each goal. For example, if you wrote down that you want to earn $100,000 in the next twelve months, you'll want to list that goal under your career or professional pillar. Remember, you decide how you want to label your pillars. I'm including an example of how I group mine below:

Financial Security

Live within my means
Save for taxes along the way with my payroll
College savings for kids—pay half
Taxes in by April 15
Contribute 10% to retirement on every sale
Reserve savings full
Quarterly taxes paid on time
Credit score up another 20 points
Update car

Life Mapping Institute—*Live Your Gift*

Life Mapping Institute Facebook page
Live Your Gift Companion Guide
Book manuscript draft complete March 31
20 hours per week for writing
Meet with Dr. Pillay in Boston
Competitive landscape complete
Book published by December 31
Book proposal written by April 30
Landing page for workshops
Set book launch date

Physical

Body fat to 17 percent or under
Workout: cardio 2x week, walk, yoga, stairs, etc.
Train with weights & trainer 3x week
Nails every two weeks
Pedicures every two weeks
Facial 2–3x per year
Dysport 4x per year

Brows 6x per year
Cut and color with Gabe every 5 weeks
Blowouts for special occasions 4x per year

Creature Comforts

Clothes shopping
New couch
Emerald-cut diamond ring
White purse
Jewelry: earrings, bracelets, necklaces
Work skirts (4)
White business tops (2)
Black boots, thicker heel, round toe
New brown and black belt
Peep-toe pumps
Re-cover dining room chairs
Lulu pants (2)
Thick pearl bracelet
King-size duvet

Family

Travel to Boston
Build a new home or remodel in downtown
Weekend getaways: Alderbrook & Seabrook
Build a waterfront home
Touch base with kids regarding homework and grades
Family picture with professional photographer in Hawaii
Travel to a country outside the U.S.
Provide opportunity for YoungLife Camp
Eat together as a family at least 3–4 times a week
Kids helping with 100 mailings per week

Symphony, ballet, theater four times a year
Vision boards with kids in January
Cook with boys; teach them how to cook
Schedule Hawaii trip
Seahawks game
Fishing, regular or fly

Career

Business Facebook page live—Land to Luxury
Five Star logo on email signature
Marketing plan for Kirkland new construction Facebook page
Send 400 mailings or emails of value every month
Average sales price is $1.2M and higher
Work my weekly calendar with time blocking
Website refresh
Plan this year's Alderbrook Retreat
Darren Hardy High-Performance Forum
Contacts 100% up to date and then 2x per month
Auto-emails monthly
Sell a lot for a $5M new construction listing in Kirkland
Five Star Profile complete
Update testimonials
Create buyer/seller testimonial sheet
On-site photos for new construction

Spiritual

Personal growth videos/podcasts/Audible weekly
Take walks along the lake once per week
Flowers at house, fresh, twice a month or more
Cooking classes
Read books that expand my knowledge (4 per year)

Two charity auctions
Counseling monthly
Embellish paintings
Self-acceptance; work on body
Writing my book
Writer's workshop
Youth Mental Wellness Task Force
Public speaking
Daily practice of evening visualization
Daily gratitudes and idea book in bathroom
Read daily meditation
Journaling

Prioritize Your Goals

Once all your goals are separated into their respective pillars, it's time to prioritize them. First, identify every goal you hope to accomplish within the next twelve months. Then identify the top two to four goals from each category that you'll specifically focus on in the next quarter. Finally, choose the top three most important goals overall. Don't worry; we'll continue to return to this list of goals for future action and continue to reprioritize them. You will work toward the other goals when your schedule permits and after you complete your short-term focus goals. Once you cross one goal off, you'll insert another in its place.

Start by asking yourself, "Which goals will propel me forward in my life, in my career, and with my family in an impactful, positive direction?" You're looking for goals that will make a significant difference if accomplished in the next thirty, sixty, or ninety days. We need to prioritize goals so we don't put the cart before the horse.

One example I can give you is regarding my work. I'd really like to have a systematic marketing approach for how I stay in touch with my sphere of influence every month. I'd like to have a monthly automated email and postcard delivered, as well as make weekly social media posts related to my business. Automating my marketing is an important goal. However, I am also in desperate need of upgrading my contact management system. Launching an automated marketing solution with inaccurate client information is both ineffective and a wasteful use of marketing dollars. Updating my contacts should absolutely come first. It's my highest-priority work goal I have over the next thirty days.

Over the years, I've found it works best if I choose priority goals with a thirty-, sixty-, or ninety-day time frame while working toward the larger goal, which may take a year or longer. Tracking progress feels more manageable and motivating in shorter increments. We'll be monitoring our action steps frequently. Working on priority goals gives us the ability to gain laser focus.

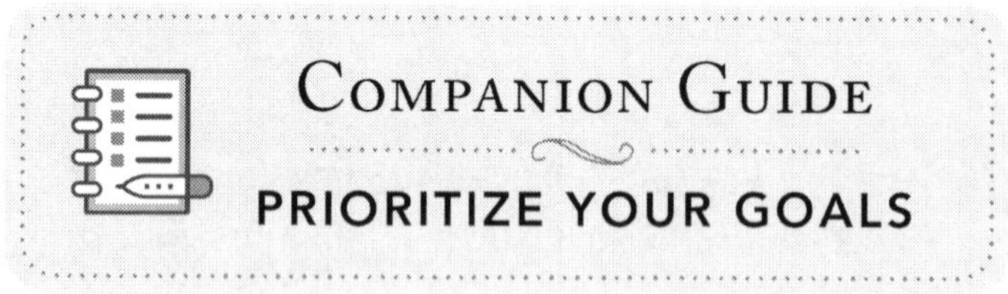

It's time to read back through your pillars and prioritize your goals. First, mark all the goals you'd like to accomplish within the next twelve months. Next, highlight the top two to four priority goals from each list. Finally, highlight the top three overall goals you are most excited about working on. If you have trouble narrowing your list to three, you'll want to select goals that will catapult you down the path for the most impactful, significant change in the short term. When you look back three months from now, what goals will lead to reduced stress, positive momentum, increased income, and a real sense of accomplishment? Consider choosing at least one personal goal rather than having all three from one category. However, you are the captain of your ship; choose your coordinates carefully.

A Sample Priority Goal List

Here is a sample priority goal list with three focus goals bolded.

Spiritual

Find a church this year.
Write my first book.
Read books or listen to an Audible book four times or more weekly.
Take a class to learn to paint.

Family Goals

Eat dinner together as a family a minimum of four nights a week.
Plan quarterly college tour trips.
Plan Hawaii trip with the boys.
Attend boys' sporting events.

Physical

Weight-train three times a week; do cardio two times a week.
Eat clean during the week and enjoy a few indulgences on the weekends.
Get manicures twice per month.

Career Goals

Update database twice monthly.
Implement an automated marketing program.
Sell ten lots this year.

Security/Financial

Save for taxes with each commission.
Contribute 10% from each commission check to retirement.
File annual tax return and quarterly tax payments on time.

Creature Comforts

Update my car this year.
Purchase a new duvet cover for the master bedroom.
Purchase a new briefcase for work.

A Quick Review

This is a good time to review the differences between beliefs, principles, values, and goals.

Our Beliefs List represents the universal truths and why we believe we're alive. Our behavior is the living example of our Principles List. Values are the things that make our lives more enjoyable and the reason we have the goals we do. Goals are what we're striving to achieve, learn, or acquire to support our core values.

When you look at my Priority Goal List, you will find "Write my first book." The core value this goal supports is "integrity." I've known for several years that I'm meant to be writing as an expression of my gifts. Since I've had this awareness but wasn't taking action, I didn't feel I was living in integrity. The principles I am following are as follows:

1. I will listen to and honor my inner voice.
2. I will challenge myself by always having a willingness to learn.
3. I will share my story with others.
4. I will do things I am fearful of as a practice of showing up "big"in the world!

These are all behaviors in support of my belief that by living in alignment with my soul, I will experience a heightened sense of joy, and by listening to God's guidance, I'm honoring His purest intention for my life. Here's one final example in a visual format:

GOAL ALIGNMENT

Goal	Body fat at 17%
Value	Physical, spiritual, and emotional well-being
Principle	I will keep my body at its optimal health by staying fit and eating 85% clean.
Belief	I believe it's my responsibility to lovingly care for my body, my soul's earthly vessel.

Now that you've identified your top three priority goals, we're going to ensure our minds are primed to go from point A to point B.

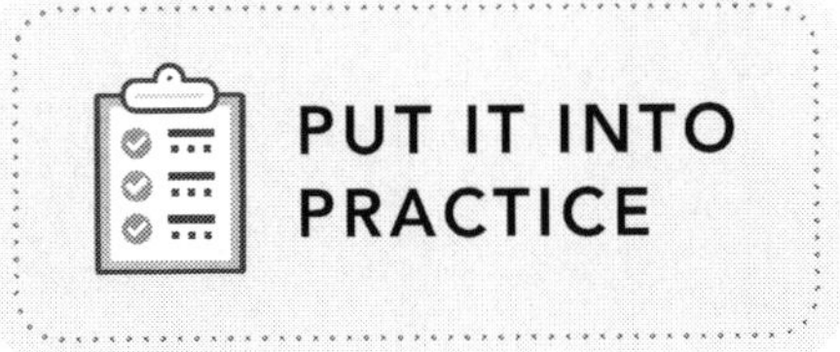

CHAPTER SIX

Your Magnificent Mind

"When I dare to be powerful, to use my strength in the service of my vision, then it becomes less and less important whether I am afraid."

—Audre Lorde

Living Their Gift

Joanne was clinically depressed and unable to believe she would ever feel good again. She had separated from her husband, whom she had married only thirteen months before, and left Portugal to move closer to her younger sister. With an infant daughter to care for and no means to support her, she signed up for welfare benefits. She described her situation as being "as poor as it is possible without being homeless."

Just a few years earlier, her mother had passed away after a ten-year battle with multiple sclerosis. Joanne had watched her mom's health deteriorate daily from an aggressive form of the disease, and when she died at the age of forty-five, Joanne was greatly impacted by the loss.

A failed marriage and raising a child in near-poverty added to the grief over her mother. She became preoccupied with death and mortality, even contemplating suicide. Instead, she turned to completing a story she had started before her mother's death.

Writing had always been a source of comfort for Joanne. She had written her first story at age six and had always wanted to be a writer. Over the course of the next year, her ideas took shape and the manuscript was completed in 1995. It was the first in a series of seven books that would electrify the publishing world and send millions of young boys and girls running to bookstores for the latest installment about a school for wizards.

J. K. Rowling is one of the most celebrated authors of our time. Her *Harry Potter* series has shattered sales records and has been turned into some of the highest-grossing movies of all time. What endears her to fans around the globe is that she is completely authentic. She has openly shared her past struggles and is not ashamed to have admitted to being depressed. As she said, "What's there to be ashamed of? I went through a really tough time and I am quite proud that I got out of that."

What is also inspiring is that she is a champion of living our own story and not someone else's. While most of us aspire to be the next celebrated achiever, she encourages all to be something even better: "to be the first *you*."

To be the first you. To be authentic.

J. K. Rowling is living her gift, and the impact she has had on millions of lives is immeasurable. Her belief in sharing the story of a young boy's journey after the loss of his parents—born of her own grief and pain—has allowed younger generations to thoughtfully discuss the meaning of life and the inevitability of death.

And she reminds us that in creating our own stories, the goal in life is not perfection. "Perfection is unattainable. Instead, aim to seize the moment and push through the hardship. Dare to follow your dreams even, or especially, when things are tough."

> " We do not need magic to transform the world. We carry all the power we need inside ourselves already. "
>
> —J. K. Rowling

Envision and Achieve

The imagination and creativity J. K. Rowling displayed in her books is simply astounding, made all the more remarkable by the fact that as she had written them, she had been consumed by overwhelming grief and a fear of failure. And her story—not Harry's, but hers—is a powerful one because it shows how the mind can dictate the course of action in our lives—either engulfing us in pain and limiting beliefs or fully unleashing our gifts. *Harry Potter* is more than a fantasy series for children; it is a beautifully woven series that serves to help children, and many adults, understand loss, treasure friendships, and always remember that there is magic inside us.

So how do we find that magic to create the world we desire? It starts with identifying the roadblocks in our lives, training ourselves to overcome our limiting beliefs, reframing our thinking, and using a little creativity to put us on the path to our authentic self.

Over the years, I've become an observant student of myself. What I mean by this is that I frequently notice my thinking, self-talk (both good and bad), wandering mind, behaviors, conversations, and emotions. It's as if my own little angel spirit is flying over my right shoulder and hovering about a foot away from my head. Usually, when I'm sharing this with people, I raise my right arm automatically and my hand moves in a circular motion in the open head space. It's in these moments of self-examination that I'm reminded I'm still a work in progress, and always will be.

Time affords us invaluable insight and perspective into our past. As a perfectionist, I'm always evaluating, discerning, critiquing, and sometimes affirming my thoughts and actions as I move through life. Over time, patterns emerge. One pattern I became curious about was my inaction on certain goals I wrote down. Several times a year I read through my 100s List to highlight the things I've accomplished. However, I began noticing certain goals were not only incomplete, but that I hadn't even taken a single step to start them. Feeling annoyed by this realization, I remember sharing my observation with my real estate broker, Mike Connolly.

Mike is a lifelong student, and although I know he wanted to help me, he didn't have the answer. He was curious about it, too, because in his role as owner, designated broker, manager, and coach, he has seen this pattern with his agents time and again. His agents have lofty numbers attached to sales goals at the beginning of the year only to fall short, often by a lot, at the end. I decided it was time to start doing a little investigation into the actual science behind motivation and goals, self-sabotage and procrastination, and goal achievement.

I never questioned whether or not there was concrete evidence behind the idea of envisioning a goal and achieving it. Since I was raised by a mom who desperately wanted a different life and reality than what she had, it was ingrained in me that these concepts she shared were facts! Plus, one thing we knew not to do in our house was question authority. So I took her word as truth and internalized concepts like affirmations, visualization, associating certain colors with positive outcomes, and vision boards. My mom started reading about our ability to influence our thoughts and outcomes back in the sixties. This was back when many of these concepts were considered "woo-woo" and "new-age"; even today they aren't universally accepted or practiced. Fortunately, the rapidly expanding academic fields of neuroscience, neuroplasticity, and quantum mechanics continue to reveal the power of the magnificent human mind.

Several studies point out the importance of how we formulate our goals. Discovering there's a right and wrong way to set goals was somewhat of a relief to me. It wasn't that I hadn't had my share of success over the years; I had. However, where my soul is concerned, it was deeply troubling to me that I wasn't taking action on the goals I felt would be truly meaningful to me.

The purpose of this chapter is to highlight the most relevant scientific evidence in support of our journey to becoming the best we can be. The following topics are intended to provide awareness, information, and tools, as well as support effective implementation of your life map.

I like to think of the systematic approach of life mapping as pulling together all the necessary ingredients to make a colossal ice cream sundae. Up to this point, we've determined what we believe, how we want to show up, what we value, and where we'd like to put our focus. Now that we've decided on our favorite flavor of ice cream, it's time to add a little personality by decorating our sundaes with our prefered toppings. The following toppings strengthen, reinforce, and bring clarity to the vision we hold for our goals. This is where our uniqueness mixes to create a one-of-a-kind masterpiece. In this chapter, we'll discover several best practices to support the achievement of our goals. Here are some of my favorite toppings, but this is in no way an exhaustive list.

Limiting Beliefs (Hot Fudge)

I'm not a therapist, but I can tell you from experience that limiting beliefs are a show stopper. Much like the thick, gooey, sticky consistency of hot fudge, slathered all over a child's face after devouring an ice cream sundae, our limiting beliefs cling to us long after their usefulness wears off. Typically, as we grow from children to teens and into young adulthood, we adapt to our environment by developing certain coping mechanisms. While some may have been useful for our survival in our family of origin, some stick with us and no longer serve us in adult life.

Identifying limiting beliefs is a crucial step to remove roadblocks. These self-defeating thoughts lurk where they silently, secretly, underhandedly sabatoge our best intentions. You may be aware of some of these beliefs. There may be others you don't yet recognize are running the show in the background. When I bring awareness (also called mindfulness) to my self-talk, I can usually uncover what these nasty limiting beliefs are saying to me.

One personal example I can share with you is in regard to writing this book. I mentioned earlier how I felt I was being nudged toward writing and I'd received several signs. As I like to say, God was speaking to me. His message was loud and clear. At first, it was a subtle whisper ("Pssst."). Next, it was more like a friendly clap ("Hey you!"). Then an attention-grabbing crisp finger snap ("Did you hear me?").

Finally, there was a startling high-pitched whistle like a seasoned New Yorker uses for hailing a cab ("Phreeeeet! Dana, I'm not playing games here. I know you heard me. I'm not going away!").

Other messages came in the form of visions and encouraging phrases. They were overwhelmingly positive. I didn't question their authenticity or where they were coming from, even though I had no idea (and still don't) what the final outcome will be. But even with a spiritual belief that I was being guided, I mentally swatted the messages away.

When I get quiet and ask myself what that's about—why I consciously ignore what I deem to be reliable, loving, guiding signals—this is what comes bubbling up: "Dana, do you really think you have something to say that people will want to read? There's no way you have the ability to take on one more thing; you're already spread way too thin. What are you thinking? Writing? Speaking? Dana, are you crazy? You're responsible for feeding your boys! You can't afford the distraction! Oh, you really think you're going to be some notable author? Ha!"

Ugh. Isn't that terrible? I have so much empathy when I see others who are hurting, stuck, or beating themselves up. Sadly, I haven't afforded myself (up until recently) the same comfort, understanding, nurturing, and encouragement. The old limiting beliefs don't belong with me anymore. They don't belong with you either!

Limiting beliefs feel like sheets of thick gauze wrapped round and round our bodies. Suffocating, isolating, and stifling, these layers of fear paralyze us until finally we realize we have the power to transform and to shed the layers of our old selves just like butterflies emerge from their cocoons. Every one of us miraculously possesses the power to retrain our thought patterns. Our brains are truly remarkable this way.

A big part of personal growth is recognizing where we're still stuck. We must do the work. If we don't, old thoughts will sabatoge meaningful change. We'll be left wondering why we didn't do what we said was so important. When we call our secrets out of the darkness, we relinquish their control. I'm a firm believer in studying anything that helps us better understand ourselves. Whether we want to stop unhealthy patterns, heal old pains and traumas, improve our current relationships or our way of thinking, there are many resources available to us. No one is going to rescue us from the hole sinking our ship. We are our destiny's captain and we must take responsibility for making ourselves as healthy as possible. I'll always advocate for seeking professional help from counselors or psychiatrists. If you feel you are stuck in cement or quicksand, please do yourself a favor and ask for help and work through it; there is a way out.

To continually better ourselves, I believe we must let go of the notion that there's a final destination. What if the destination is simply living as the best version of ourselves throughout our journey? If we surrender to being present and do the work, we can focus on experiencing life today instead of someday. Having goals gives us hope and direction for our future, but it shouldn't preclude us from living and enjoying our todays. I'll always have something I'm looking ahead to, but I also remind myself it's OK to notice and appreciate exactly where I am today.

Here is a list of questions to contemplate prior to identifying specific limiting beliefs related to our goals. This list of questions is meant to bring awareness to areas we may not realize are impacting our lives. If you discover anything that brings up a lot of emotion or feelings of sadness, anger, or frustration, please consider engaging with a professional who can help you work through those feelings:

- What patterns are still reoccurring and taking space in your thoughts? For example: poor body image, anxiety about the future, feeling unloved, resentment, addiction, holding on to past grievances, or not fully engaging in relationships.
- Do you have a "less than" mentality in any areas of your life?
- Are you waiting for someone to rescue you?
- Do you love and accept yourself as you are?
- Is there anything from your past preventing you from being fully present in your life now?
- Are there reasons why you think you may not be worthy of accomplishing this goal?

Reframing (Oh, Nuts!)

Reframing means intentional practice nurturing our brain's thought patterns. It may be introducing new positive self-talk or strengthening the internal wise voice that's always been there. If you are someone blessed with an eternal outlook of positivity, I genuinely envy and admire you! I see your lightheartedness and I appreciate your ability to always find the light, especially when I'm dragging. Unfortunately, I'm not one of those people wired that way . . . yet! I know a handful of people who naturally exude this healthy default. They're my inspiration. I love how naturally positive people emit lightness, happiness, and confidence. We know it's impossible to experience sunshine and rainbows all the time, but you know some of the happy people I'm describing. They're one step ahead in projecting a brighter outlook and I'd love to learn to emulate their energy.

I'd much rather practice resetting my brain's default chatter to positive, loving, and supportive words than continue listening to the crap that was seeping out. (Which I had done until recently.) I've learned that the word *yet* and phrases like *up until now* or *until recently* are great ways to put my brain on notice that something's about to change!

Daily Practice (Rainbow Sprinkles)

We need a daily practice to positively rewire the default self-talk because those old defaults were at work for a long time. All of the tools suggested in this chapter will assist with that goal. However, I think it's important to note that without regular practice, the likelihood of an overnight miracle or meaningful change . . . well, it just isn't likely. Fit people don't have toned muscles by randomly picking up a dumbbell and repping out a few curls throughout the week. Instead, people who care about their health block out time to go to the gym and train regularly. Similarly, a more naturally positive state of mind requires discipline and practice.

A morning practice such as *The Miracle Morning* by Hal Elrod or a morning ritual are all the buzz right now and for good reason. Practicing a daily routine to center ourselves is a great way to set the tone for the day. Logically, doing it first thing in the morning makes sense, but logistically it doesn't work for everyone. If mornings are tough, I think it's better to find a time that works for you rather than not having the habit at all. That's why I refer to this tool as "Daily Practice."

Some of the more popular suggestions are reading a daily inspiration or devotional, reading or reciting a religious passage, praying, meditating, journaling, writing affirmations, focusing on goal visions, reading affirmations, practicing gratitude, stretching, or doing yoga. The possibilities are endless.

Consider the environment where you'll enjoy your daily practice. Choose somewhere you feel good, lifted, inspired, grounded, energized, and comfortable. Some will light candles, turn on soft music, or peacefully enjoy absolute silence.

The Daily Practice is meant to be a time free of distractions so you can focus on you—not your phone, your kids, significant other, work, email, Facebook, or laundry. This time is for you!

It's time to think about what we'd like our Daily Practice to look like or if it's possible to improve the one you already enjoy. Answer the following questions:

- What activities would you like to incorporate in your daily practice?
- How much time will you spend?
- What time of day will you schedule your daily practice for?

Affirmations (Mini M&Ms)

Affirmations are positive phrases or paragraphs, stated repeatedly, describing your desired outcome. A positive affirmation is structured as if we've already accomplished the goal. Our subconscious cannot decipher between the future and now, so we program it to believe what we are saying is true. We can do this by writing the affirmations down, saying them out loud, or silently thinking about them. Repetition creates new brain chemistry and opens us up to attract what we desire. Here's an example of my first-version affirmation about this book:

I feel a tremendous sense of pride in writing *Live Your Gift*.

It's positive, stated as if it's already completed, and includes a feeling of pride. That should be good enough, right? Not so fast. After pouring over the research related to the formation of affirmations, I realized that there's a lot more than meets the eye.

Lana Hall, a psychologist quoted in an article called "The Science Behind Self-Talk," recites three primary reasons why affirmations are important:

1. If we are reciting affirmations to ourselves regularly, it's more likely we'll demonstrate behavior to support what we say we want.
2. It activates the "goal-seeking mechanism" in our brain. We'll suddenly become aware of opportunities or ideas to support our focus goal. It's also giving ourselves permission to "'unfocus" so we can attract what is still unknown.
3. We reconnect with our core values, where we have a much stronger belief in ourselves. Reinforcing a belief that we are achieving our goal (desired outcome) triggers our reward center and allows us to maintain our "possibility mind-set."

A 2002 study by Drach-Zahavy and Erez informs us that we must believe we are capable of achieving our goals in order for the affirmation we write or recite to be effective. Our goals also need to be challenging. That's how we'll get the best results from ourselves. We need to pause and ask if these two things are present in our focus goal *before* we write out an affirmation. Otherwise, we set ourselves up for self-sabotage and feeling worse than when we started. If we don't quite buy in to the stated goal, we can reformulate it until we do.

Not only should you put the goal in a positive light, but when the goal is tied to our fundamental core value(s) it has far-reaching effects (as discussed in Chapter 5 on Goals). The reason looping the goal back to a core value is important is because our strongest, naturally confident sense of self resides in our values. Not only does this relationship give us a comprehensive understanding of why our goal is truly important, but our resilience increases by insulating us against setbacks. We may not have reached the goal's final destination, but we will be more apt to push forward knowing we have a strong value underlying our goal. (When we get to the Goal Inquiry Form soon, we'll be asking ourselves which core value this goal supports.)

No doubt we'll come across unexpected challenges. That's just life, right? If we hedge our goals against our values, we will bounce back more quickly and dramatically increase our odds of accomplishing what we originally set out to do.

Next, grab your camera because you're the director of the next Hollywood blockbuster movie. Your detailed vision, pinpoint clarity, and creative artistry infused throughout the storyline greatly increase the odds of your production being Oscar worthy. As you bring your goal into focus, engage all of your senses: sight, smell, hearing, taste, and touch. How will you feel? If you're not entirely sure, think of a time in the past when you enjoyed a similar type of accomplishment. What emotions will you experience? (Our subconscious allows us to attach prior experiences of positive emotion to the goal in our sights.)

How will accomplishing this goal improve your life? Are there people around to support you? Where are you? What do you see, hear, smell? Write it all down. In addition, as you imagine what the scene looks like achieving your goal, experience it happening through your eyes. It's best if you are in the vision versus watching yourself from outside. In other words, it's better to be the actor experiencing the manifestation rather than the director.

One final suggestion on affirmation. It was mentioned multiple times that being our own personal coach is beneficial. What I mean is there's evidence suggesting if we talk to ourselves, out loud even, it's an effective form of motivation. Gary Lupyan, assistant professor of psychology at the University of Wisconsin, found "naming what you're looking for out loud—for example, 'keys, keys, where are my keys?'—helps us to keep the visual representation of the object in mind." It would be like Roger Bannister warming up before his big race and giving himself a pep talk by saying out loud, "Roger, you've got this! You know you can break the record!"

We'll experience sustained, far-reaching, positive effects for creating detailed affirmations and visualizations, effects that will extend well beyond accomplishing the goal in focus. The process of self-affirmation makes us feel good and, therefore, if we practice the technique regularly, those positive effects will stay with us long term. It reinforces what we value, improves our overall sense of well-being, and improves our ability to regulate emotion. The cumulative research uncovers a template for constructing the most effective affirmations, which I think is exciting. As we gain more insight from neuroscience and goal achievement research, we'll continue to fine-tune implementation strategies.

Affirmations have come a long way since I started writing mine down almost four decades ago. I've enjoyed the past year being a student sifting through dozens of research papers, analyzing blog posts and media stories, and talking with past participants of my workshops. After distilling the information, I believe I've uncovered a best-practices guide for creating what I'm calling "Value-Focused Affirmations."

Here's version two of my affirmation about writing the book. It emerged after meditating, after "tinkering" with intuitive hits (flashes of vision, messages I've heard from God, along with an unquestionable trust in my intuition), after daydreaming, after allowing my imagination to wander freely, and while deep in the process of writing. If you're reading this, then I'm happy to say that at least some of what I envision is materializing.

Dana's value-focused affirmation for writing *Live Your Gift*:

> "I'm empowered and humbled by my courage to act on writing my first book. The manuscript was turned over to the copy editor on time, and the first print run of the book and *Companion Guide* were delivered before the end of the year. Accomplishing this goal means I listened to God, my intuition, and my visions, which support my belief that my life is for continually learning and playing "big" in the world. My guiding principle of stepping into the fear means I'm demonstrating my core value of integrity. This includes my personal integrity and allowing my boys to see me accomplish this goal, and most importantly, honoring God's highest intention for me by living my gifts. The vision I hold is this: I'm standing on stage behind a podium, in front of hundreds of people who are applauding, smiling, and nodding at my acceptance of an award for my writing. Happy people, full of poise and gleeful laughter, dressed in classy, black-tie formal attire and evening gowns, seated around beautifully decorated round tables draped in black and white linens and adorned with brilliant white floral displays and flickering candles, enjoying a divine five-course dinner, are celebrating everyone being honored tonight for their accomplishments. I am full of gratitude, grace, and joy to be here accepting my award. I'm truly blessed to be living a life in alignment with my soul."

I can honestly say, that's the first affirmation I've ever written that made me cry. There's something about sharing it openly that feels vulnerable, truthful, and courageous. Not everything makes complete sense to me as I complete the final draft of the book. However, this is an example of me trusting my gut, my intuition, and what I believe is a result of God's nudging, which started many, many years ago. This reminds me of something I read in Brené Brown's bestseller *Daring Greatly*. The title of her book comes from this passage written by Theodore Roosevelt. It's commonly known as "The Man in the Arena."

> "It is not the critic who counts; not the man who points out how the strong man stumbles, or where the doer of deeds could have done them better. The credit belongs to the man who is actually in the arena, whose face is marred by dust and sweat and blood; who strives valiantly; who errs, who comes short again and again, because there is no effort without error and shortcoming; but who does actually strive to do the deeds; who knows great enthusiasms, the great devotions; who spends himself in a worthy cause; who at the best knows in the end the triumph of high achievement, and who at the worst, if he fails, at least fails while daring greatly, so that his place shall never be with those cold and timid souls who neither know victory nor defeat."

I'm daring greatly and you can, too.

Read your affirmations daily. There's no set rule, but we learn through repetition. I read mine in the morning and at night. I have them written out, laminated, and posted in my bathroom to read when I brush my teeth. I know I'll see them at least two times a day since I always stand in the same place, so I don't even need to think about it. Walk through your daily routines and decide what will work best for you. Certainly, whenever you are frustrated or thinking of giving up on your goal, I'd recommend reading your affirmations as well as the Goal Inquiry Form (we'll talk about this soon). Doing this will put you in touch with your feelings and reinforce your thought process when you created the goal.

Many people also make a daily habit of writing down their affirmations. The mental process of thinking about your affirmation and then translating the thoughts by guiding your pen to write down the words is reaffirming and deepens learning and memory more than just reading something out loud.

Creativity (Yogurt Chips)

Children bring a wonderful sense of adventure and awe to the world. Controlling norms of society and time spent in the world slowly drain this playfulness and delight from most of us. But there are a few who are lucky enough to escape childhood with them still intact. The rest of us must consciously look inward to where our playful, childlike innocence hides. You can start by asking yourself, "When do I laugh, smile, and feel at ease? What am I doing and who am I with when I feel happy and playful?"

Adam Werbach wrote an article titled "Three Little Words" for the *Sierra Club Bulletin* in which he tells of a group of researchers who asked a preschool class, "Who knows how to sing?" Every child eagerly responded that they could. "Who knows how to dance?" Same response. "Who knows how to draw?" You guessed it; every child responded positively. The following week, the researchers were asking the same questions of the students at an elite university. "Who knows how to sing?" A few responded that they could sing. "Dance?" Two reluctantly responded. "Draw?" Not one hand.

Somewhere between preschool and college, most of us think we've lost those abilities. How do we lose them? Are we letting society slowly drain them from us with each negative response to our own individual expression of who we are? Are our children losing their abilities, or are they losing their confidence in their abilities? Artistic endeavors are but a small sampling of the gifts taken from us as we grow up (but do we ever grow up?). A child's world is full of curiosity and excitement. We can benefit by reconnecting with this playfulness inside of ourselves. Allow time to explore your creativity. It requires patience, gentleness, and a willingness to invite our childlike spirit to reemerge—but it's so worth it! When we give ourselves and others permission to be authentically who we are, our gifts will rise as a blessing to the world.

I discovered a brilliant mind with a deeply caring spirit when, by happenstance, I came across the work of Dr. Srini Pillay. Dr. Pillay is the male version of Brené Brown, PhD. (If you're not familiar with Brené Brown and her TED talk, The Power of Vulnerability, it is one of the most viewed. She researches shame and vulnerability and is passionately committed to helping people live wholeheartedly.) They both generously share what they've learned as academic researchers by courageously revealing the human implications of their findings in lay terms. Dr. Pillay is an assistant professor of psychiatry at Harvard Medical School, an author, a keynote speaker, a master certified executive coach, and the CEO of NeuroBusiness Group. Dr. Pillay is passionate about "brain-based personal development" and empowering people to maximize their potential.

Mike Connolly, my broker, whom I mentioned earlier, is an avid reader. In 2012, Mike told me about a book he thought I would enjoy called *The Answer* by John Assaraf and Murray Smith. He was right; I liked it a lot. It was my first formal introduction to quantum mechanics. Assaraf and Smith used quantum research to support the book's message for creating a wildly successful business. Fast-forward to 2015 when I was preparing for our first office overnight retreat. As I was searching the web for articles related to "self-sabotage and procrastination," I came across a company owned by John Assaraf called NeuroGym. Several videos popped up on his site. One was a 2012 video of Dr. Srini Pillay called "How and Why Your Fears Are Holding You Back."

Early in the video Dr. Pillay posed the following question to the audience: "How many of you would like to live an exceptional life?" Of course, everyone raised their hand. Then he shocked them by telling them, "By definition, an exceptional life is a life of low probability." I think almost everyone sunk down in their seats and the air was sucked right out of the room. Luckily, he followed that up by saying, "So unless you want to live a life just like everyone else, you need to throw probability out the window." Instead, he offers "possibility thinking" as a catalyst to goal achievement.

After following Dr. Pillay's videos for a few years, I was eager to read his 2017 book, *Tinker Dabble Doodle Try*. The book is loaded with interesting statistics from brain research studies and easy-to-follow suggestions to ignite brain creativity. He teaches all about the power of accessing our "unfocused mind." By consciously switching from focus to unstructured "downtime," we invite numerous benefits from better health to laser focus when we really need it. His book is like a dictionary defining specific techniques to experiment with "tinkering, dabbling, doodling, and trying." He believes "unfocus" is the key to freeing up "a possibility mind-set" locked up in our overly focused brains.

One practice that helps me let go and allows my mind to wander is a meditation called "Your Future Self." I like it because lots of images come to me. The sound of the storyteller's voice soothes me into following her guidance. During these ten minutes I time-travel to visit with a vivid seventy-year-old image of myself. The dreamy scenes that emerge are inspiring, encouraging, and sometimes surprising. I trust the process and welcome what I am called to notice. I lose my agenda, free-float, imagine my future, and usually some part of my current direction becomes clearer. I say usually because this doesn't happen every time. The art of meditation is releasing any expectation of the outcome and simply letting it unfold.

There is an endless supply of guided online meditations, meditation apps, and styles of meditation. Dr. Pillay talks about mindfulness meditation, which focuses on the breath. Of course, your mind will drift off, but the object is to "gently ignore your mental chatter" and bring your mind back to your breath. It has powerful effects on lowering stress and anxiety while also allowing our minds to be open to receiving. Dr. Pillay is convinced when we come back to structured focus, we will be much more on task.

Dr. Pillay's recommendation is up to seventy-five minutes of focused activity for the first session of the day, followed by a fifteen-minute break. Subsequent concentrated blocks should be around forty-five minutes followed by fifteen more minutes for brain play. (He makes a point to say that these are suggestions and there is no one-size-fits-all.)

It doesn't take long to disengage from concentration. In ten to fifteen minutes, we can take a walk, catnap, draw, listen to music, play an instrument, meditate, cook, sing, dance, or engage in any other activity where we lose ourselves. I'm still a beginner in this concept, but I am actively practicing it while writing this book. I'm using a timer with focused work projects and attempt to shut down and shut off any potential distractions (the ringer on my phone, turning my phone over so I can't see it lighting up when I receive a text or call, closing the email and Facebook apps on my computer, etc.). I have noticed I feel a little more relaxed when I come back to writing or my work.

Early in the book, Dr. Pillay points out that dementia and Alzheimer's may in part be due to not spending enough time accessing this creative side of our brain, and that certainly got my attention. If the outcome of playing a little more is lowering the odds of suffering from a terrible mind-altering condition or disease, I'm all in.

Dare to try new things! It's unlikely you'll regret the effort!

Companion Guide

UNFOCUS

Let's think about how we'll cultivate more creativity and "unfocus" in our days.

Vision Boards (Gummy Bears)

Making a vision board is fun. If you're excited about your goals for the year, this should be something you're eager to get started on. There's incredible energetic reinforcement from having a visual illustration of your goals. A vision board stimulates our sight and shines a mirror on what we want most. It's a great place to highlight your top-priority focus goals and keep them in the forefront.

There are a few important elements to include on your board, but primarily, this exercise is *your* creative expression. There is no one right way to design a work of art, and I personally think vision boards are beautiful works of art! Four of the components were suggested to me some thirty-five years ago, and the other is from current research.

Things to include in your vision board:

Include a reference to your Higher Power

It can be what you feel is appropriate based on the beliefs you listed. This is the way we acknowledge that our goals are achieved not only through our focused efforts but also with universal support.

Include lots of pictures

We're lucky we have the internet. If you don't find what you're looking for in magazines, you can simply search online and, voilà, you'll have the perfect image. I've used pictures from brochures, magazines, and newspapers, as well as online images and actual photos. The nice thing about searching on the web is that you can adjust the image to any size you like. You can also use a copier to enlarge or minimize anything you find in print.

Use lots of descriptive words

Words help reinforce the feelings and emotions your goal elicits. The words can also describe the goal itself. For example, double my income, travel, love, trust, accomplishment, family time, confidence, peace, yoga, New York City, waterfront home, and so forth.

Be specific

Here is an example: Let's say you want a new car, a Mercedes, specifically. You find the word Mercedes while flipping through a magazine. Cut it out and then also find a picture of the exact model and color you'd like to have. The combination of words and images is more powerful than just words or pictures alone. Likewise, if you want the goal accomplished by a certain date, make sure that's on your board.

Include supporting core values

If the goal of doubling your income supports your value of financial security, then choose an image that defines security. This could be a copy of your bank statement, with the bank logo. You could white-out the current balance and write down what the new balance will be when you double your income. (Like affirmations, your vision board is "as if" you've already accomplished your goal and you are now living it.) You could tape a dollar bill on your board or a rainbow with a pot of gold.

How often should you make a vision board? That's really up to you, but I will typically make one every year. Just as your values may shift, your goals will shift too and, therefore, your focus for what you're trying to achieve. Several of my workshop participants make their vision boards 100 percent online. They use Pinterest to gather photos and words and then arrange the layout to their liking on another document.

We experience a deeper level of cognitive learning when working with our hands versus a computer. I'd encourage you to make your vision board the old-fashioned way with scissors, glue sticks, and poster board. However, if it's the difference of making one and having a visual aid to support you versus not, then by all means, use your computer. When you're finished, be sure to print it out. You don't want your gorgeous visual creation hidden in a folder on your computer. Place it in areas where you'll be reminded and inspired by the benefits of achieving your goals.

If you create your board the old-fashioned way, I suggest taking a picture and making a few color copies so you can see it often. I keep an extra copy of mine in my daily planner right next to my life map.

How and when will you create your vision board? Make a note of the supplies you'll need and where you'll go to get them. Invite family or friends to make one along with you. It's a great project to work on in the evening while you're watching TV, over pizza with another family, or with friends or co-workers. Jot yourself a note in your *Companion Guide* or calendar and block out the time.

Color (Whipping Cream)

Color imagery and the correlating physiological and emotional effect is predominantly studied in marketing. Big corporations invest a lot of money researching implications of color in branding and advertising campaigns. They have one shot to gain consumer acceptance, and that leaves little room for error. Missing the mark with their target consumer may translate into millions of dollars in lost revenue. These are huge line items on their overall annual expense budget. Consider that a thirty-second clip for Super Bowl LII was $5 million!

My strong bias for surrounding our visions in color comes from personal experience. My belief in the power of visualizing with color began when I was a young teenager. My earliest recollection is when I was about thirteen. It was a spring Saturday and I was waiting for my name to be called for an audition. My mom was right beside me and we were sitting on those cold, hard plastic classroom chairs with metal legs outside the theater door in an empty high school hallway. The historic school had been converted to a community center and housed the rehearsal studio for the prestigious Pacific Northwest Ballet, Seattle Children's Theater, and a few other community-based nonprofit organizations.

Auditioning included reciting a three-minute monologue in front of judges who would select the kids to participate in a summer theater program. It was spring of my seventh-grade year and, if selected, I would be spending eight weeks of my summer in an intensive acting program with the Seattle Children's Theater.

My mom noticed my nervousness and told me she had a suggestion to help me relax. She went on to say, "Close your eyes and slow your breathing." After a few breaths she continued, "Imagine you are on stage and seeing the judges sitting in the audience. Can you see that?" I nodded my head. Her voice was calming. It was soothing like she was a meditation guru. "Imagine you are lightly tethered to the judges from your heart to each of theirs by a long roped cord. Now imagine the cord is floating and suspended by your desire to be selected in the acting program.

"Dana, you need to realize these are people just like you. They have fears and worries, too. Now picture a soft pink light emanating from the center of your heart, shining across and through the cord and all the way over to them; this represents your heart and love for performing. It's as if the rope is an umbilical cord and they can feel exactly what's in your heart. Surround youself with white light, filling the entire theater; this represents your faith that God will be there with you, cheering you on and believing you will give your best monologue ever. OK, now that you've filled the entire theater with pink and white light, trim it off with a brilliant band of gold. Can you see it? The gold represents success and being chosen for the program. Are you imagining all of that? Good. Just hold that in your mind as long as you need to. With every breath, just relax and remind yourself, they are people just like you."

It gives me goosebumps to think back to that day. She gave such powerful advice on the days when she felt good and was engaged. I miss that. My thirteen-year-old self completely absorbed what she said. I believed her. I could see it in my mind, clear as day, and still can. It calmed me down to the point that, even though I was still nervous, I felt more in control and I gave my best performance. Thankfully, I was chosen and participated in the summer intensive.

Throughout my life when my nerves are high and my body's feeling anxious, I envision being connected by pink light. I intentionally slow my breathing and I remember that we are all the same—just people finding our way through life. Whenever I care very deeply about the outcome, my heart beats faster, and adrenaline flushes through my body. It's disorienting, as if the quickening pace disconnects me from where I feel grounded to my soul. Linking color to ground my anxiety is a helpful tool.

Have you ever used color in that way? It makes logical sense to me for a few reasons:

1. We are all unique and attracted to different colors. What may be a gorgeous shade of blue to me may not evoke the same response from you.
2. We often define ourselves by the colors we surround ourselves in: our clothing, our house decor, or the car we drive.

Color evokes emotion. We're surrounded and influenced by color day in and day out. Associating my favorite colors with visualization, affirmations, or mindfulness brightens up my vision, intensifies my connection, and infuses life into my goals. Color has the ability to positively influence our thoughts and moods.

There's some general concensus of what meanings and emotions are associated with particular colors. I've included a chart here. Use it to your greatest advantage!

COLOR CHART

White	Purity, Heaven, God, Unity, Calm
Yellow	Optimism, Communication, Creativity, Clarity
Pink	Emotions, Feminity, Romance, Innocence
Red	Fire, Power, Passion, Confidence
Green	Growth, Land, Money, Health, Peace
Blue	Subsconscious, Trust, Strength, Confidence
Purple	Intuition, Prestige, Imagination, Creativity
Black	Protection, Endings, Distinctive, Elegant
Orange	Playful, Friendly, Cheerful
Brown	Earth, Wholesome, Rustic, Warm, Natural
Silver	Sleek, Modern
Gold	Rich, Valuable, Prestigious

What are your favorite colors and how will you apply them in relation to your focus goals?

Mindfulness (The Cherry on Top)

Mindfulness includes a broad range of definitions. What it means to me is a conscious intent to notice my surroundings, interactions, and thought patterns. It's an opportunity to look at the people, places, and things we encounter on a daily basis and experience them in a very different light. When was the last time you were actually intentionally aware and observing of nature, architecture, your city streetscapes, your home, or the people you love?

Yes, I know, we see these things all the time. You may wonder, what's the point of being "intentionally aware"? It's a practice in grounding ourselves and feeling more connected to the world we live in. It's an opportunity to observe and appreciate the things we've become numb to and take for granted. When is the last time you stopped your car to gaze at brilliant fall leaves or spring blossoms? Or smiled at how your son's hair flips up so perfectly around his ear and then told him so? Or thought, my gosh, this building I work in is stunning! Or told your partner how incredibly beautiful they are to you?

Showing up to your life mindfully is beneficial for two reasons: One, it allows us to see beauty and goodness all around, even when it feels like the sky is falling. And two, it allows us to be curiously aware of our own patterns and behavior by intentionally taking a look at ourselves. Seeing our surroundings in a new light and with renewed appreciation is akin to practicing gratitude. It's refreshing, it's re-centering, and it reminds us there is so much more to life than the minutiae we are so easily swept up in. When we take the time to look beyond our tunnel vision, suddenly the picture becomes broad with depth, color, variation, and vibration. We're reminded there is a world full of people like us pushing through life. As much as we'd like to think it's all about us, there's a world full of magnificence and brilliance far beyond the outline of our shadow.

The benefits of our ability to be intentionally aware and curious toward ourselves is a blessing. We have the capacity to observe, learn, and modify our thoughts and behavior if we discover we have habits no longer serving us. Likewise, we can benefit by recognizing where our personality and character shine, so we reinforce what we do well. Unless we pause to take personal inventory, we will have awareness only if someone outside of us makes a point to tell us. And even then, I think we often discount or minimize someone else's opinion of us. Have you ever been criticized by someone and thought, "That's rude!"? Or when you're complimented by someone saying, "Wow, you are really looking fit!" you discount it by replying, "Oh, that's nice of you to say, but I've got a long way to go."

If we have an open mind-set, we are saying, "I want to learn, I want to be better, and I care about being the best I can be." Sure, it may come with a few stinging reminders of our unglamorous character defects, but the beauty is we can choose to change. The only way we continue to learn is by welcoming feedback and getting curious about where our "blind spots" are. Ray Dalio, the founder of Bridgewater Capital and author of the *New York Times* bestseller *Principles*, made it his personal and company mission to ALWAYS seek to understand what was working and what wasn't, and he would apply what he learned to ensure better outcomes in the future.

Ray Dalio is an example of a lifelong student of personal, business, and human development. When communication breaks down at his company, he seeks to understand not only why but also how to fix it. Mr. Dalio's concern is deeper than bottom-line profits. He genuinely cares about Bridgewater's culture and his goal: maximize every employee's innate skill set. Every employee is evaluated on multiple levels using psychological testing. This testing provides feedback on things like natural skills and abilities, tendencies for interacting and collaborating with others, processing of information, whether they are big-picture or task-specific focused, and whether their perceptions are intuitive or observational. In his book, he describes the meticulous skill and orchestration required to fully maximize personal and organizational effectiveness. He said it's like leading a symphony! He also makes it clear he wouldn't have it any other way.

If we want to live an extraordinary life, one in which we're continually growing, we must be willing to practice self-awareness and mindfulness, have a possibility mind-set, and surround ourselves with supportive people who want the same.

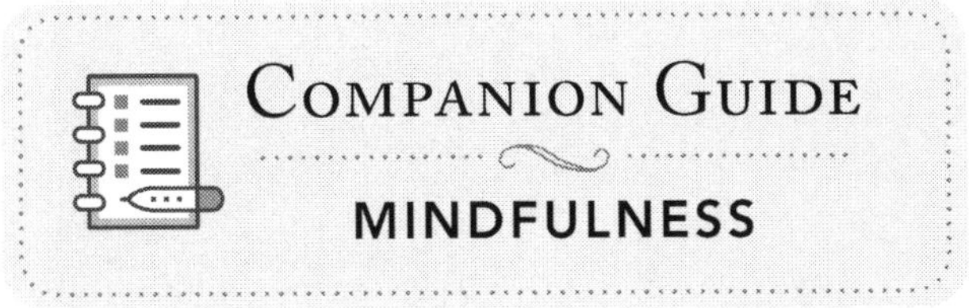

How will you practice mindfulness?

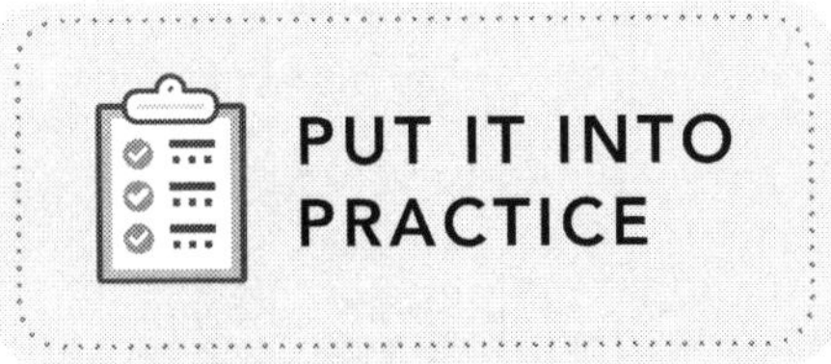

Part Two

The life mapping process

CHAPTER SEVEN

Life Mapping

> “To live is the rarest thing in the world. Most people just exist.”
>
> —Oscar Wilde

Living Their Gift

Mark's story is not unlike those of many children of divorce who, angry at the breakup of their families, wander aimlessly through their teen years and express their frustrations through aggression. In Mark's case, however, his actions resulted in arrests and a permanent felony assault record.

The youngest of nine children growing up in one of the toughest neighborhoods of Boston, Mark was left unsupervised after his parents divorced. He was eleven years old at the time, and over the next few years he dropped out of school, started hanging out with a street gang, got into drugs—developing a cocaine addiction—and turned to violence.

In 1986, at the age of fifteen, a civil action suit was filed against him for racially inspired attacks he had led. Two years later, he physically attacked two Vietnamese men, bashing one over the head with a wooden stick. He was charged with attempted murder, pleaded guilty to assault, and served forty-five days of a two-year sentence.

Mark had always looked up to those serving time in prison, including members of his own family, but earning his stripes was not at all what he had imagined. When the cell door closed behind him, he asked God for His help, vowing that when he got out, he would change the direction of his life.

When he was released from prison, he joined his brother Donnie in a new boy band; however, he left after only a few months. Over the next decade, he collaborated with rappers and had some success with his own musical act, reaching the *Billboard* 100 hit list with a song from his first album. However, it was in 1993 that his life took a major turn, with new opportunities turning him into one of the most recognizable faces in the film industry.

Mark Wahlberg, formerly known as Marky Mark in his musical days, is now one of the most sought-after actors in Hollywood. His success in movies such as *Boogie Nights*, *Planet of the Apes*, *The Departed*, and *Ted* has earned him millions of dollars and legions of fans.

As a teenager, his life path was headed for a life behind bars. His time in prison was a wake-up call that he had to change. "I wanted to prove to people through my actions—not my words—that I was going to change and that I was going to make a positive impact on the community that I come from," he said. "I could not forget about where I came from and find myself in this position without helping and giving back."

Faith was the tool that allowed Mark to turn his life around. Today he starts every day "on his knees" in prayer and attends Mass every week with his wife and four children. "Somebody came to speak at the church and asked, 'Are you a participant in the church and the community, or are you a spectator?' And I was like, 'Whoa.' I felt like, yeah, I'm a bit of a spectator right now. I'm coming and getting what I need, but I'm not really giving back, you know, reciprocating the kind of love and support I'm getting."

Today, through his Mark Wahlberg Youth Foundation, the angry young boy who had no direction in life is now helping to raise and distribute funds for youth service and enrichment programs.

> "My faith has given me the ability to be a good father, a good husband, and most importantly, a good person. Faith brings great joy to my life and my life brings me closer to my faith."
>
> —Mark Wahlberg

Inner Blueprint

Mark Wahlberg's story is a perfect example of how life mapping is an integral part of living your gift. The life mapping process takes us from where we are to where we want to be. It helps us put our lives into perspective. It takes us through the steps necessary to find the answers that lie within us. Life mapping helps us stop the noise and see beyond the superficial world of today to a life of substance with deeper, clearer meaning. We create a crystal-clear vision of the people we are destined to become. That vision will lead us to change many of the daily activities that currently define our lives. If we have been trustworthy in our actions involving others, our actions have defined us as trustworthy people. Once our activities are in alignment with our inner blueprint, we begin to live a life that we can define as authentic. Living authentically brings profound fulfillment and joy.

You might be wondering, What is an inner blueprint? It is our personal, innate plan for our lives. It doesn't change, but our understanding of it, as we age, does. The more we learn to listen and understand it, the closer we will be to living it and experiencing the rewards associated with that alignment.

Life mapping, along with working through a lot of emotional pain, led me from a life measured by possessions and status, to one of true calling, which includes connection, empathy, love, and sharing my gift with others instead of squandering it hidden in fear. The journey has not been an easy one and I believe it's continually evolving. The benefits of stepping into our true calling far outweigh looking back on life with regret.

Fourteen years ago, at age thirty-four, I was a mom with four little boys. The three youngest of those sweet boys came from my second husband and all three were under three and still in diapers! I made the mistake of ignoring my gut and core values by agreeing to design a house well beyond my comfort zone. The original plan was to build a 4,500-square-foot home. However, the actual design ended up being 7,300 square feet with a much higher price tag. The reality was we only had the income to stretch somewhere in between! I saw two options: Either sell the home as a spec (which equated to failure for me and "looking bad" to the outside world, including my husband) or do everything in my power to get my head back into work mode so we could qualify for the additional loan we needed to finish the home.

Even though we pulled it off, it all felt very "out of integrity" for me. The process of setting the goal and making it happen wasn't the problem. We did that. The problem was much deeper because my gut intuition was screaming at me, "STOP!" (That was before the excavators had even turned a mound of dirt!) Instinctively and logically, I knew the timing wasn't right. Although we had the income to qualify for the initial loan on paper, it was a stretch so far beyond anything I was remotely comfortable with that it never felt right.

It's true I enjoy surrounding myself with nice things, but spending money only feels good when I've earned the right to purchase as a result of hard work and it's within my financial means. When I make buying decisions through that lens, then I'm in alignment with my core value for financial security. That means *already* being in a financially secure position (as I define it) and then deciding to purchase or not.

Verbalizing my discomfort wasn't the problem. I did that, but at the time, I wasn't strong enough to stand firm in my "NO!" As soon as I detected what I thought was a twinge of disappointment, I translated my husband's expression to mean he was disappointed in me, and I folded. My fear of letting him down spiraled to the conclusion he would no longer love me, which meant he would leave me, which meant I would be alone . . . again! Can you see the twisted power of unhealed childhood trauma? I was more afraid of losing the relationship and being alone than trying to figure out how to juggle four kids, working full time, and having the ongoing stress of a crazy mortgage payment.

Sometimes we do need to compromise in relationships. However, in this case it wasn't simply a compromise; I was completely violating one of my primary core values: financial security. There was nothing about the home that left me feeling financially secure.

Life mapping helps us identify where our goals may be out of alignment with our fundamental beliefs, principles, and values. It's imperative that we ask ourselves why we want to accomplish a goal and if it is supported by our beliefs, principles, and values.

Here's an example of how author Bill Cohen successfully used the life mapping process.

> "In 1981 I was a manager with one of the largest insurance companies in the world. I used the basic life mapping techniques with all the people I was managing. This group of individuals rose from 50th to 1st in sales and service in our region and from 1,150th to 38th in the company over a nine-year period. This was accomplished in a manner consistent with the integrity that grew out of the core beliefs and principles of the group. We resisted the pressure to shortcut our principles in order to receive instant recognition, preferring instead to hold fast to the belief that our devotion to correct principles would prove successful in the long run. Although we were always near the bottom of the month-long promotion lists, by the end of the year we were always near the top. Our constant dedication to predetermined activities produced the desired results over the long run. Those routine activities may seem less than spectacular in the short run, but they have a compounding effect that produces extraordinary outcomes."

Bill goes on to say,

> "The inevitable result of the life mapping process practiced over time is evolution. This evolution began to change the way I related to life in general. For example, the ambition for financial success began to take a back seat to the desire to become a more fully human person. The result has been a more peaceful, contented life. The wonders of nature have now become more evident to me. I no longer have the need to constantly acquire things; sharing has replaced that passion. My relationships with my son, Josh; my daughter, Emily; and most importantly, Gail, my wife, are wonderful and grounded in love. Life mapping is the tool that has opened the lines of communication and led me to these rewarding and fulfilling relationships."

Living a life defined as successful means enjoying the journey and, at times, enduring it. We need to accept that long trips are occasionally interrupted by detours, breakdowns, construction work, and flat tires. Forward momentum may come to a screeching halt from time to time, but we can learn to accept the interruptions as a normal aspect of our journey. I firmly believe there's a reason we find ourselves on a road in life that unexpectedly comes to a dead end. Even during shock, surprise, or disappointment, we can have faith there's a better route for us up ahead.

Charting Your Course

Visualize your life as a trip into some unknown country, where every turn has three or four forks in the road. When you are born, you are given a map to follow. That map determines the place you start your journey, like the city where you are born. If nothing else influences you, you will follow the predetermined route and know which fork to take, every time. As you take your first few steps, you begin to feel the influence of your environment. The people, places, and things you encounter begin to affect your decisions. The possible routes or lives you could live become unlimited. Each fork provides a whole new series of possibilities. Now comes the difficult part. Some of those routes are filled with happiness and fulfillment, while others bring heartache and regret. How will we know which forks to take?

We can attack this problem from two basic points of view. We can accept life as it comes to us and deal with the forks as they appear (my business coach calls this "living five minutes in front of your face") or we can develop skills that will lead us toward a life that brings us the greatest fulfillment. Most live not by choice, but by default.

> "If you don't design your own life plan, chances are you'll fall into someone else's plan. And guess what they have planned for you? Not much."
>
> —Jim Rohn

Some might escape this destiny and still be happy. But most will endure a life filled with regret. This is what life mapping is all about: taking our innate gifts and using them to create an extraordinary life, the one our soul most desires.

One of the most important skills I've learned from my business coach is how to distinguish my innate personality and preferences and the difference between "front seat" and "back seat" activities. Jessica Butts is an expert on the Myers-Briggs personality type indicator and an author of two fantastic books on the subject. In her book *Live Your Life from the Front Seat*, she illustrates exactly what your personality type means by using an analogy of a car.

Jessica's naturally spunky spirit is full throttle as she describes each component of our personality type (extrovert or introvert, sensing or intuition, thinking or feeling, judging or perceiving). Everyone has an innate preference of one over the other in each paired grouping.

It's something we're born with. She associates each tendency with four seats in a car: driver and passenger in the front, and drunk uncle and the baby in the back. Each one of the sixteen Myers-Briggs types brings with it distinguishable characteristics and preferences.

I mention this because I think it's invaluable to understand who we are and why we naturally show up in the world the way we do. Jessica is the first person I've heard describe the results in a way that was meaningful to me. The images I have of my "baby in the back seat" crying and "drunk uncle" barely able to keep his eyes open make it super easy to recognize when I'm doing something I shouldn't be. I now understand why some activities come so easily for me while others are like nails on a chalkboard. The information on personality type is complementary to the work we do in life mapping, especially if you've been struggling in your career.

Where Do Our Choices Lead Us?

It is easy to be fooled into thinking that having fun is our chief aim in life. We may think when we are wealthy enough, we will finally have a good time! But fun without *purpose* soon loses its allure. Fun is what makes the journey enjoyable, but the journey must have a worthwhile objective for it to have any real meaning for most of us. Goal-setting theory shows that people who set challenging but achievable goals report being happier than those who have responsibilities that are deemed too easy. When we understand what our true purpose is and start living that journey, we will not need to worry about having fun along the way.

Most of us need help recognizing our unique talents and gifts. Will a completed life map help us? Of course it will! Can you imagine heading off to visit your best friend at her new home in an area you've never been before without a GPS? The directions are indispensable, right? A map provides you with a variety of routes from which to choose. You might pick the most direct route, the one with the least traffic, or the most scenic for your journey. The odds of reaching your friend's home and enjoying the trip are substantially increased if you have confidence in where you're headed.

A life map is a snapshot of your life at a specific point in time with your best route identified. There will be changes and modifications along the way; life is in a constant state of evolution and flux. Embracing the life mapping process, embodying its philosophies, and incorporating specific daily exercises will facilitate lifestyle adaptation. This isn't a quick fix. It's a process and is akin to a chronic dieter learning how to live a life free from dieting. We say goodbye to the yo-yo, inconsistencies in what we say we're going to do, and hello to the freedom to choose a life of balance and fitness. We immerse ourselves in a proactive, healthy lifestyle in which we determine our direction and say goodbye to stagnation and self-imposed suffering.

We all want to be successful. Most of us were born with that trait. One of the problems we have in achieving good results is defining success for ourselves. A life map will help us define our meaning of success. It will unlock our inner resources. A life map is our personal outline for reaching our unique destiny. The life mapping process will take you through the steps necessary to determine what really matters to you. Sadly, most of us spend too much time doing things we don't really want to do instead of living life doing all the things we love!

Great achievements are built on a solid foundation of dreams. They are created in the mind first, on paper second, and finally in the daily activities that lead to their accomplishment. Wise people take their dreams for tomorrow and begin living them immediately. You can't wait for the perfect situation before you start. "Perfect" is a mirage and all we are assured of is today!

Which will you choose? Develop a life map of your future and begin living it today or accept life as it is with regret for what you didn't accomplish? These are two very different paths. I hope you will join me on the road to living your gift.

> "Sometimes the people with the greatest potential often take the longest to find their path because their sensitivity is a double-edged sword—it lives at the heart of their brilliance, but it also makes them more susceptible to life's pains. Good thing we aren't being penalized for handing in our purpose late. The soul doesn't know a thing about deadlines."
>
> —Jeff Brown

Turning Inward and Looking Within

Your life map begins by exploring your imagination. Instead of focusing on everything and everyone around you, you are invited to discover *your* world. You will learn to define yourself and your ideal role in the world. This part of the process requires you to understand your own belief system, the list of principles (behaviors) you believe you should follow, and your current core values. Why is this important?

Most of us would describe ourselves as truthful. When we lie to others, we define ourselves as liars. Our conscious mind may hold on to the false opinion that we are truthful, but our subconscious mind discerns the deception. We have created a conflict. That conflict works to destroy the foundation our life is built upon. We think less of ourselves, and our subconscious mind begins to sabotage us. If we make a habit of lying, we begin to find lying less and less painful, until one day even our conscious mind concedes, and we begin to rationalize that it's acceptable because everybody lies. It is acting in direct conflict with our beliefs that starts this negative spiral downward. Keeping our actions in line with our beliefs is at the heart of the life mapping process. What are the steps for living in harmony with our beliefs?

Life mapping is a multi-stage process:

1. Determine your beliefs.
2. Develop your list of ideal behaviors.
3. Identify your core values.
4. Identify what brings you joy so you can experience more of it.
5. Make a list of your goals.
6. Prioritize your goals.
7. Choose your highest-priority goals.
8. Break down the goals into activities.
9. Create a practice for a healthy mind-set.
10. Design your ideal schedule.
11. Build structure and accountability to ensure success.

You may be thinking, "Wow, this is going to require a lot of work!" Guess what? You're right. If you've ever been told nothing good comes easily, they were telling you the truth. These steps are all necessary for progress, growth, and sustained forward momentum. I've already been there and done that trying to take shortcuts, and it doesn't work. I'm providing this groundwork for you in hopes that your journey will be much smoother than mine. Until I incorporated ALL the steps into my lifestyle, my accomplishments were hit-or-miss at best. Mostly, it was miss. I certainly wasn't internally rewarded when I stopped challenging myself. I know when I'm capable of more, so I was letting myself down! Anyone who is an amazing athlete learns they cannot expect to go up to bat and assume they'll hit a home run. Batting averages go up when training is steady and intentional. We will reach peak performance only after we decide we are ALL IN!

Once you develop your life map and start your new journey, you will occasionally want to drive into the service station for a tune-up.

Check under the hood to make sure you are not creating conflicts with your inner blueprint. Staying true to your life map makes it easier to set healthy boundaries when others attempt to pull you off course and lure you to an easier, faster route. News flash: There isn't a faster route! People may attempt to influence you by trying to convince you that their wants are more important than your true needs. It's important to have conviction for what you want to achieve. Your goals and aspirations may not be in line with people who currently surround you. If what you say you want is truly important, you must make it a priority to connect with people and groups who offer encouragement and support and share the same interests as you.

Your persistent actions will ultimately lead you to achieve your goals. The excitement and challenge you experience will inspire you as you start to reveal the person who's been hidden inside. As you begin living your life map, your vision of the future will emerge with more clarity. If you have been walking in a dense fog, your sense of direction and purpose will crystallize, allowing you to pinpoint exactly where you are headed. You will see the adjustments you need to make to improve your quality of life. Life is one continuous journey. Therefore, your life map is an essential tool. It's a living document, and not a goal in and of itself. You will regularly recalibrate your coordinates as unexpected twists and turns compete for your time and attention. But now, *you are in charge* and *you* have the power to decide how you'll respond. One day you will look back in awe at how far you've come. Your life map and the beautiful landscape that results will ground you through life's challenges. You will have the strength to thrive despite unforeseen circumstances!

Finding Our Path

I don't want to change you into my vision of you. Rather, I want to encourage you to embrace the person you are called to be. It may seem overwhelming at first, but soon the activities you practice will become habits and it will be easier to stay on your new path than to go back to the old. According to Thoreau in *Walden*:

> "I learned this, at least, by my experiment; that if one advances confidently in the direction of his dreams, and endeavors to live the life which he has imagined, he will meet with a success unexpected in common hours. Why should we be in such desperate haste to succeed, and in such desperate enterprises? If a man does not keep pace with his companions, perhaps it is because he hears a different drummer. Let him step to the music which he hears, however measured or far away."

Thoreau wants us to understand that living the life we imagine might be different from what those around us expect of themselves. Have the courage to follow your convictions, take your time to find your path, and success will surely follow.

CHAPTER EIGHT

Activities

> "Do not wait; the time will never be 'just right.' Start where you stand, and work with whatever tools you may have at your command, and better tools will be found as you go along."
>
> —Napoleon Hill

Living Their Gift

Elon was the victim of what far too many children today must unnecessarily endure: childhood bullying. Born in Pretoria, South Africa, he was consistently bullied throughout his school years. In one instance, he was left unconscious after a group of boys threw him down a flight of stairs and beat him senseless.

At the age of seventeen, he moved to Canada to enter university, and then to the United States, where he received a bachelor's degree in physics at the University of Pennsylvania and another in economics from Wharton School of Business. At age twenty-four, he was accepted into a PhD program at Stanford but left after two days to start his own company.

Elon had always been a daydreamer—and an intellectual daydreamer at that. He envisioned a world with self-driving cars, renewable energy, and artificial intelligence. His interest in outer space led to the idea of private space exploration and the colonization of Mars. Where NASA believes the technology to transform the red planet into a habitable environment is beyond our grasp, Elon disagrees, arguing that there is the ability to terraform the planet to make it more Earth-like.

Elon Musk has not been deterred from those who snicker at his lofty goals. And he has never been deterred from grasping at the future to bring new possibilities closer to us in our lifetimes. The creator of PayPal and the founder and CEO of both SpaceX and Tesla, he has amassed a fortune estimated to be nearly $21 billion. He continues, through the development of innovative technologies, to preserve and expand human consciousness to defend against any threat to our survival.

Elon has not been without his hits and misses in his quest for space exploration or in his other business ventures. In fact, he nearly went broke at one point and resorted to living off loans from wealthy friends.

But he has not let the failures stop him from taking the steps necessary to advance his dreams. And he approaches each new idea by making sure it is solid in its foundation before moving on to the details.

"I think most people can learn a lot more than they think they can. They sell themselves short without trying. One bit of advice: It is important to view knowledge as sort of a semantic tree; make sure you understand the fundamental principles—that is, the trunk and big branches—before you get into the leaves/details or there is nothing for them to hang on to."

While Elon is somewhat notorious for setting ambitious deadlines he often cannot meet—as most of us are prone to do—he does not let that affect his goal. As he says, "Better to do something good and be late than bad and be early." The point is he does not give up. He sticks with his plans and does not let outside interference, or any internal negativity, deride his intentions. He is living his gift of bringing the future to us one step at a time, and the future through Elon Musk's eyes looks exciting.

> "I think it is very important to have a feedback loop where you're constantly thinking about what you've done and how you could be doing it better."
>
> —Elon Musk

Laying the Groundwork: Ready!

Elon Musk applies a "scientific method" to every new idea—tried-and-true steps that will allow him to lay the groundwork for a plan and then keep it moving forward. He does not let failure deter him, and he keeps faith in the process.

Likewise, the activities you do every day define you, your character, and your contribution to this world. Some people mistake activity for achievement. They are so busy doing things, they don't have time to evaluate the results of all that activity. It is not just any activity that leads you to achieving your goals; it is a particular set of activities.

Activities without goals are like aimless darts, and goals without activities are dreams; when activities and goals are interconnected, everything is possible! Your Beliefs List tells you *why* you are alive, your Goals List tells you *where* you want to go in life, and your Principles List and Activity List tell you *how* you will get it done.

This diagram shows an example of how beliefs lead to activities.

Belief	I believe I have an ability to make a positive impact on other people's lives.
Principle	I will work hard and be financially rewarded because of my hard work.
Value	Financial security
Goal	Complete rebranding for work: Land to Luxury™.
Activity	Over the next 90 days, I will invest four hours per week toward my goal.

The achievement of our big goals requires us to consider a few things prior to identifying all the necessary steps. We need to know the parameters that define our ability to achieve the top-priority goals we selected. Completing this discovery will prepare us for what's ahead.

The first step to goal implementation is to be thoughtful in our approach. We need to prepare just like the farmer tills his soil before planting the crops. Now that you've decided which goals you'll specifically focus on, it's time to learn about the Goal Inquiry Form. This worksheet will help you gain clarity on the positive intentions surrounding your priority goals as well as identify potential roadblocks. You'll uncover your reasons for choosing the goal, what it will allow you to do, and what your biggest obstacles may be. You'll isolate any associated limiting beliefs and devise a plan for reframing deflating thoughts into motivating, healing, and reinforcing wise words to empower you. Finally, at the end of the form, you'll write out your vision statement, and this will become your value-focused affirmation.

Goal Inquiry Form: Get Set!

On pages 151–152 is the Goal Inquiry Form that we will be referencing in this section. I fill out the form before starting work on any of my top-priority goals. Every ninety days I review my progress from the previous quarter. Once I complete a goal, I identify the next quarterly priority goal. This is an added step, but it's well worth the time. We'll cover each question on the form line by line here. Note that you can visit www.lifemappinginstitute.com/resources to download this form.

1. **Priority goal:** What is the priority goal you'll be focusing on?
2. **Date today:** The date you are completing the form.
3. **Completion target:** The date you hope to have the goal completed.
4. **Why is this important to you?** Write down the reason you believe accomplishing this goal is important.
5. **What will it allow you to do?** Write down what you think accomplishing this goal will allow you to do.
6. **Biggest obstacle?** Write down the biggest obstacle standing in your way of accomplishing this goal.
7. **Is there a skill you need to acquire?** Write down if you need to learn any new skills to accomplish this goal.

8. **Will anyone be impacted while you work on this goal?** (Check one.) ☐ YES or ☐ NO
9. **Who?** Write down who will be impacted.
10. **Do you need to get their buy-in?** (Check one.) ☐ YES or ☐ NO
11. **If so, when will you have a conversation with them?** Write down the on or before date you'll talk to the person(s) who will be impacted by working on your goal.
12. **Date completed:** Write down the date you spoke to whoever will be impacted and check the box.
13. **What structure do you need to increase your odds for success?** Write down what type of structure will support you in your pursuit of this goal.
14. **Is there a fear associated with achieving this goal?** (Check one.) ☐ YES or ☐ NO
15. **If so, what's the fear?** Write down what you are most afraid of or concerned about if this goal materializes. This may seem counterintuitive since this is a goal we're saying we want to focus our attention on and will forward our lives by accomplishing it. The reason we name the fear is because "Affect Labeling" is shown to provide numerous physical and psychological benefits around what's causing us stress. This allows us to feel more in control. When we are in control, the emotion is not controlling us.
16. **Preemptive strategies or resources to put the fear at bay:** Write down what you'll do to give yourself extra support and accountability.
17. **Do you have limiting beliefs to call out?** (Check one.) ☐ YES or ☐ NO
18. **If so, what are they?** Write down all the little or big things that the nasty doubter voice says to you. You may need

to think about this for a bit. Consider other times you've attempted to work toward a goal and you didn't complete it. What messages were you getting about yourself?

19. **Do you know where the limiting belief comes from?** (Check one.) ☐ YES or ☐ NO
20. **If so, where?** If you know where the limiting belief(s) came from, acknowledge it. Usually it's from a time when we were very young. If you can pinpoint where it originated, it will help diffuse its power.
21. **Wise words to reframe:** Write down the positive, nurturing phrases, words, or mantra you'll use to knock down doubts when they creep in. It's highly likely you will experience moments of fear, frustration, and uncertainty about the goal you're striving for. We want to equip ourselves with tools to deflect these old, negative, no-longer-useful limiting beliefs. This is where we exert our power to reframe our thinking and rewire our neuropathways. What would your eighty-year-old wise self say to encourage you today?
22. **What one daily practice will you do to reinforce your wise words?** Write down the activity you will do at least once a day to strengthen, practice, and focus on your priority goal. When will you do it? How will you do it? What will you do?
23. **What core value does this goal support?** Write down the core value, or values, you'll support by achieving this goal.
24. **How does it support the core value?** Write down how achieving the goal will support your core value.
25. **What positive emotions will you experience?** Write down the feelings you'll experience when you achieve your goal and while on your way to achieving your goal. If this is a big stretch goal for you and you've never done something like this before, think of other accomplishments and the positive

emotions you experienced. You can attach those same "good vibrations" to this focus goal.

26. **Have you ever experienced these emotions before?** (Check one.) ☐YES or ☐NO
27. **If you have experienced these emotions before, when?** And, if not, think of another accomplishment where you felt similar emotions. Our subconscious allows us to link similar positive emotions to how we think we'll feel accomplishing this goal.
28. **Do you feel you are capable of accomplishing the goal as stated?** (Check one.) ☐YES or ☐NO
29. **If not, how can you alter your goal?** You need to believe you are capable of accomplishing the goal. Therefore, if you don't genuinely believe it's possible, you'll want to alter the goal until you do.
30. **How will you be accountable?** Write down how you will stay accountable to yourself and this goal. How often will you check in? Review what you've written? Who else will you check in with regarding your progress?
31. **Value-focused affirmation:** Write down the vision of yourself accomplishing your goal. Where are you? Who are you with? What does it look like? How do you feel? What are you wearing? When is it? Utilize all your senses: sight, sound, touch, taste, and smell. Describe it with as much clarity as possible, framing it in a positive light, as if you've already accomplished your goal. Name the core value(s) your goal supports. When you're finished writing your affirmation, check the Date Completed box and write the date.
32. **Crack the boulder:** On the Activity Tracker you will list all the steps necessary to reach your goal. Cracking the boulder is chiseling away at the overall size of your goal to wind up with manageable, pebble-sized activities. When you're finished

completing the form, check the Date Completed box. Write in the date you finished cracking the boulder.

OK, I know what you're thinking. This is a lot to think about. It's going to take time. It's deep, right? Yes, it's deep! It's emotional and it should be because we care. When we get in touch with what matters and realize there's garbage littered in front of our path, it sucks the air right out of us. But by doing this work, we're supporting ourselves to be everything we're capable of. It's completely normal for this exercise to bring up feelings. There's nothing easy about staring the unglamorous parts of ourselves and our past square in the eyes. It's time to call it like we see it, so we can move past being stuck. This exercise gets easier every time we do it. Considering it's made all the difference between taking action and not, accomplishing my goals versus just talking about them, I'm a major believer in the process.

Brené Brown describes digging into what gets in our way in her book *The Gifts of Imperfection*. She tells a story of being asked to speak at a women's networking lunch early on as a new author and public speaker. The woman who was introducing her didn't really know the nature of Brené's work but when she heard she was a "shame, vulnerability, and fear" researcher, she demanded Brené only "talk about the how-to-fix-it part, and not about the things that get in the way."

The woman told her to keep it light and breezy because that's all the audience wants to hear. Then she said, "Oh, and don't mention the word *shame*." Brené was completely taken aback. Yes, even a shame researcher can be hit with a shame storm. Five years later, she shared the story with her husband, Steve, for the first time. (That's how much shame she felt after derailing her own talk at the urging of someone who didn't even know about her work.) This is what Brené had to say about the experience and her realization:

"The second that I finished telling Steve the story, I felt different. I finally got it. My work—the decade I've spent doing research—it's all about "the things that get in the way." I'm not about the 'how-to' because in 10 years, I've never seen any evidence of 'how-to' working without talking about the things that get in the way. . . . Don't get me wrong, I'd love to skip over the hard stuff, but it just doesn't work. We don't change, we don't grow, and we don't move forward without the work. If we really want to live a joyful, connected, and meaningful life, we *must* talk about the things that get in the way."

I'm passionate about exposing things that stand in our way and I deeply care about you not becoming emotionally paralyzed because of past hurts you've endured. If I can shovel my way through mudslides, you can, too!

Complete one Goal Inquiry form for each of your three focus goals. Please take the time necessary. This work is about advancing your life and experiencing breakthroughs instead of breakdowns. This form sets the stage for where you're starting so you have the full picture of where you're going, and actually get there. This process is preparing you for success. You are capable of accomplishing truly great things!

GOAL INQUIRY • PAGE 1 OF 2

1.PRIORITY GOAL:

2. TODAY'S DATE:

3. TARGET DATE:

4. Why is this important to you? __________

5. What will it allow you to do? __________

6. What will be the biggest obstacle? __________

7. Is there a skill you need to acquire? __________

8. Will anyone be impacted while you work on this goal? **Yes** ☐ **No** ☐

9. If Yes, who? __________

10. Do you need to get their buy-in? **Yes** ☐ **No** ☐

11. If so, by when will you have a conversation with them? __________ 12. Date completed: __________

13. What structure do you need to increase your odds for success? __________

14. Is there a fear associated with achieving this goal? **Yes** ☐ **No** ☐

15. If so, what's the fear? __________

16. What will you do to put the fear at bay? __________

Life Mapping Workbook

live your gift

GOAL INQUIRY • PAGE 2 OF 2

17. Do you have limiting beliefs to call out? **Yes** ☐ **No** ☐

18. If so, what are they?

19. Do you know where they come from? **Yes** ☐ **No** ☐

20. If so, where?

21. What 3-5 nurturing phrases will your wiser self say instead?

22. What's one daily practice to reinforce your wise words?

23. What core value(s) does this goal support?

24. How does it support your core value(s)?

25. What positive emotions will you experience?

26. Have you ever experienced these emotions before? **Yes** ☐ **No** ☐

27. If so, when? And if not, think of another accomplishment where you felt similar emotions:

28. Do you feel you are capable of accomplishing the goal as stated? **Yes** ☐ **No** ☐

29. If not, how can you alter your goal so that you do believe you are capable of accomplishing it?

30. How will you hold yourself accountable?

31. Next Step: Write your Value-Focused Affirmation **Done** ☐ DATE:

32. Next Step: "Crack the Boulder" **Done** ☐ DATE:

Crush It: Go!

Goals are like boulders, and activities are the chunks of rock that break off when earth pushes a massive boulder from the edge of a hillside onto the earth below. Sometimes the rocks are still too large and heavy to pick up with two hands, so you may need a pick hammer to break it up into smaller rocks and pebbles. You've chosen your top three priority goals and it's time to break them into designated lists. I call this exercise "Crack the Boulder." Make sure you keep breaking the activities into smaller and smaller pieces, until each activity can be completed within a week, and then preferably a day.

The Activity List you create for your goals will morph over time. We'll discover new steps we need to take and eliminate others. Until we dive into the process of working toward our goal, we'll have blind spots. We're unconsciously incompetent (we don't know what we don't know) until we suddenly become aware. Once we're aware (consciously incompetent . . . we now know what we don't know), we can make adjustments to bridge the gap. We may need to study, conduct research, learn a new skill, or enlist the help of someone who's proficient in an area we're not. Our lists will grow as we gain clarity for what's next.

Don't get stuck on the activities; keep the goal in mind. When you plan and review each week, you will have the opportunity to change specific activities as needed to reach your goals. There will be activities and stages in pursuit of your big goals you don't like. Search for an alternative method, but don't let it be the reason you stop pursuing your goal. Darren Hardy, best-selling author of *The Compound Effect* and *The Entrepreneur Roller Coaster* and former publisher of *SUCCESS* magazine, warns that we probably won't like what we're doing 95 percent of the time. Part of the victory in accomplishing our goals is having the grit to push through.

The single most common error in developing goals is overcommitting. People get caught up in trying to do it all. The result is a schedule that is so full we feel stressed out most of the time and we are less efficient. It is better to start with less and then add to our schedule than overcommit and lose our composure or fall ill.

Once we tackle one task, we can move on to the next. Dreams and wishes will materialize with planned activities. Activities need completion dates to propel us toward our goal. In other words, we need deadlines—yes, deadlines! Deadlines provide incentive and help us develop a timeline. Studies prove their effectiveness to create a "time control mechanism" and increase the motivational impact of the goal. Activity becomes measurable and allows us to visibly see our progress, which inspires us to keep moving forward.

It's time to Crack the Boulder! I love this worksheet. Maybe that's because I'm a huge believer in lists, but this is truly my saving grace when it comes to keeping my thoughts organized. My brain is always working on something, so I fully utilize these lists to unload my thoughts in a sequential manner.

When I'm starting out on a new focus goal, I'm not ready to put dates by every item I've listed. That's OK. As you work your way through the activities, you'll logically determine what's next and attach dates. The "next right thing" will appear and rise up on your list. Writing down as many tasks as you can think of and then setting deadlines is an ongoing cycle.

Let's go over the form, and then you can start breaking down your priority goals. You can visit lifemappinginstitute.com/resources to download this form.

1. **List the focus goal:** Write down some or all of your value-focused affirmation.
2. **Does the goal fit the basic requirements of a worthy focus goal?** Is it important? Is it achievable? Is it elevating? Is it challenging? And, does it support your core values?
3. **Target date:** This is the date you're planning to complete the goal. Usually, these focus goals are thirty-, sixty-, or ninety-day goals.
4. **Actions:** This is where you brainstorm and continue to break down every item into smaller and smaller pebbles. Boulders reduced to rocks, rocks to pebbles, and pebbles to tiny grains of sand. Goals that seem massive become much more managable once we identify the smallest activities.
5. **Target date:** When you have clarity about which task you'll start with, begin setting completion dates.
6. **Actual date:** Fill in the date you finished the the task. This is great for bringing closure to the list as well as creating an opportunity to acknowledge all you are accomplishing.
7. **Check boxes next to each line:** Once you're finished, check off the box! Celebrate and be mindful of your wins along the way.

To give you an example, I counted nine pages of activity sheets for my book at the end of the first quarter. Originally, I started with close to three pages after Cracking the Boulder the first time, but as I moved deeper into the project I continued to uncover dozens of additional requirements. In addition, I kept two pages for books and articles I needed to read, one for quotes I needed to research, as well as "parking lot" sheets. My parking lot is where I'd download ideas I had regarding tasks I knew I wouldn't be covering until the first draft of the manuscript was complete. It's better for me to download all my thoughts than have them tossing around and taking up space in my head.

Follow this procedure for all three priority goals you have selected. The lists are designed to help us by setting our sights on what needs to be accomplished so we can choose where to start. The journey of pursuing our goals is part of our voyage. It ebbs and flows; it sometimes follows a straight line but usually is a winding road. Give yourself grace to be nimble and flexible and to adapt to your needs at the time. Notice the progress you're making and allow yourself time to celebrate how far you've come.

"Around here," said Walt Disney, "we don't look backwards for very long. . . . We keep moving forward, opening new doors and doing new things because we're curious . . . and curiosity keeps leading us down new paths." Walt Disney created what others laughed at as impossible. Allow your inner wisdom to guide you; it will lead you exactly where you're meant to go.

Review your Activity Lists often!

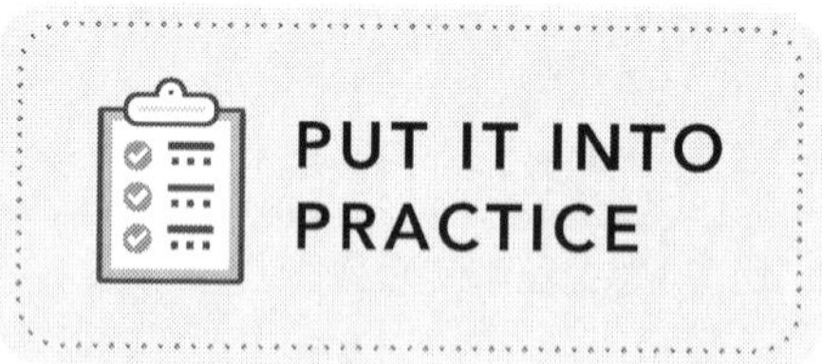

Keep Moving Forward

When your behavior or activities conflict with your intention, the correct response is to acknowledge it, devise a plan to minimize the possibility of repeating such conflict, and then move on. Don't spend another minute thinking about it. It's history.

Here is Ralph Waldo Emerson on the subject:

> "Finish every day and be done with it. You have done what you could. Some blunders and absurdities no doubt crept in; forget them as soon as you can. Tomorrow is a new day; begin it well and serenely and with too high a spirit to be encumbered with your old nonsense. This day is all that is good and fair. It is too dear, with its hopes and invitations, to waste a moment on the yesterdays."

Routines Are Good

Routines are formed through repetitive action. Unfortunately, until activities become ingrained, and sometimes even after they become ingrained, we need checklists or reminder alerts to ensure we are accomplishing everything we set out to.

If you're required to do an activity only once, don't worry about establishing a habit. However, if you will be doing it hundreds of times over your lifetime, take the time to think it through. Write down the steps involved. When you think you have optimized the activity, make it a habit! Practice by using your checklist every time you do the activity until you can do it without looking at the list. Keep the list; you might need a refresher next year.

Think of it as baseball's spring training. It's impressive to think that professional baseball players, the best in the world at their game, get together for two months to practice the fundamentals before each season starts. We should do no less if we want to become the best person we can be.

Delegation

Now, what about the activities we don't like doing that are required? You learn to delegate them to other people. What's that? You don't think anyone will do them as well as you? Then teach them. Have confidence in them and take every opportunity to encourage and acknowledge their efforts. It isn't a complicated process. You explain their responsibilities in enough detail to allow them to complete the activity. Make sure they know you have confidence in their ability and then move out of their way.

There is nothing more frustrating than being given a task but not the autonomy to accomplish it. For example, if you ask your employee to reorganize a filing system without giving him the ability to buy the needed supplies, every time he needs something he will be coming to you. That shows you don't trust his judgment and it will weaken his confidence for future decisions. However, if you give him the authority to buy whatever he needs, he will complete the task and be ready for the next one.

After a task is completed, compliment the job he did. If there's something that needs improvement, guide him. "Over the years I have become convinced that every detail is important, and that success usually accompanies attention to little details," says John Wooden, the college basketball coach with the most NCAA championships ever, in his book *They Call Me Coach*. "It is this, in my judgment, that makes for the difference between champion and near champion."

What About Failure?

What activities are required to reach your goals? Some of them will be uncomfortable. You can't stay in the same rut and still expect to reach new goals. Do you recall the insightful words of Dr. Srini Pillay? Wisely, he said, "By definition, an extraordinary life is one of low probability." Becoming uncomfortable is part of expanding and pushing ourselves to grow, and it's possible we may stumble and fall. Failure is an opportunity to learn and another opportunity to succeed. It's all in how you choose to look at it. I'm sure J. K. Rowling looks back on her most trying times and feels intense gratitude for her drive to persevere. Julie Zellinger, in her *Huffington Post* article, shares this about Rowling:

> "The author's story is practically the stuff of legends. . . . She was a struggling single mother on welfare and faced 12 rejections from publishers, eventually selling the book for the equivalent of $4,000. The series went on to break numerous sales records, it turned into an incredibly successful film series and earned a permanent place in the hearts of children and adults all over the world. J. K. Rowling is now worth an estimated $1 billion."

Rowling said her rock bottom became the bedrock on which she built her life. She knew her situation couldn't get any worse. She held on tightly to her two greatest loves, her daughter and writing stories. Pursuing her passion and utilizing her gifts lifted her out of her deepest despair.

People who are willing to make the effort necessary to fulfill their dreams deserve a lot of praise and acknowledgment. Some people, however, want results without effort. Life doesn't work that way. If something comes too easily, it usually goes away just as easily. Do you know the story of the chimp who puts his hand into a candy jar? He wraps his hand around a fist full of candy, only to discover he is unable to get the candy out of the jar because his fist is now bigger than the opening. He won't let go of the candy and consequently never tastes it. All the monkey had to do was make a minor shift in his thinking and he could have enjoyed the candy, one piece at a time.

Patience and Faith

A farmer doesn't plant a crop on a Wednesday expecting to harvest on Thursday. The farmer prepares the soil, plants the crop, and waters and fertilizes regularly. All the while, the farmer has faith that months later there will be a crop to harvest. You are preparing the soil by completing your life map. The activities you do over the next few months are planting the seeds, watering, and fertilizing. They will produce results, if you have the faith and persistence of a farmer. The farmer wouldn't forget to water the fields, even though they show no sign of growth. You shouldn't forget to do the activities you've determined are necessary for the accomplishment of your goals, even if there are no visible signs of progress. One day you will find yourself in the middle of harvesting the rewards you have dreamed of your whole life.

Darren Hardy is someone I consider a business coach. His vantage point as publisher of *SUCCESS* magazine provided him unprecedented access to learn from the brightest business minds in the world. Darren harvested all of that knowledge from his own experience and thousands of other great achievers and packaged it into his best-selling books and high-impact training programs. My friend and accountability partner, Cheryl Nygaard, introduced me to his DarrenDaily mentor videos a couple of years ago. (If you're not familiar with them, you should definitely visit dd.darrenhardy.com.)

Darren delivers a free short video mentoring session to my email every weekday morning. Watching it is one of my daily practices to get myself centered. He's thoughtfully prepared, he's direct, and he gets straight to the point. He condenses valuable information into just two or three minutes. The message of his book *The Compound Effect* is that small actions repeated over time add up to big changes. Likewise, the time and effort we spend on initially preparing our soil and planting our seeds creates a force that's difficult to stop. He refers to Newton's Law of Motion. You remember, an object at rest will stay at rest and an object in motion will stay in motion unless an unbalanced force interrupts to stop it. Newton's Law translates to our pursuit of our priority goals. Once we put in all the hard work, time, and effort (Darren likes to say blood, sweat, and tears) we're eventually rewarded by the momentum helping to carry us forward. The resulting energy rewards us by lightening our load.

CHAPTER NINE

Scheduling

> "The key is not to prioritize what's on your schedule, but to schedule your priorities."
>
> —Stephen Covey

Living Their Gift

Darren's childhood was hard core. His parents divorced when he was just eighteen months old. His mom left him with his young, ill-equipped dad, a football coach whose parenting style Darren described as a military drill sergeant and nowhere near a helicopter parent—the overprotective type who constantly hovers over their child.

When Darren was six, he went skiing with his dad and little sister in Tahoe. He spent the entire day skiing and didn't fall once. Overcome with joy by his accomplishment, he ran to tell his father the news. The response he received left him stunned.

Upon hearing that his son had not fallen, Darren's dad said, "Well, then you didn't get any better."

Little Darren stood there in silence until his father said, "Look, Darren, if you don't push yourself past your current ability, then you can't grow. You have to fail to improve. Falling is part of getting better."

Throughout his childhood, Darren was constantly reminded of his dad's philosophy on life: no pain, no gain. In fact, that mantra was painted on the garage wall. Like the drill sergeant he was, Darren's father made sure that the lesson was drilled into Darren's psyche every single day.

Darren Hardy is a self-taught serial entrepreneur whose determination, perseverance, and enviable work ethic have propelled him to great heights in the business success industry. Over the past twenty-five years, he has run three successful television networks, was the founding editor and publisher of *SUCCESS* magazine, and has become a *New York Times* bestselling author. His books—*The Compound Effect, The Entrepreneur Roller Coaster,* and *Design Your Best Year Ever*—have helped millions of people who want to go beyond their current level of success.

Sharing the secrets of success with those striving to be better is Darren's full-time priority. And he is a prime example of reaching

for one's full potential. Many people believe that Darren's powerful stage presence and impassioned speaking are natural gifts. However, Darren attributes 99 percent of his mastery to hard work. In a *Forbes* interview, he stated, "You are the creator of your destiny. The mind-set of 'they were born to be successful and I am not' is a trick of the imagination. The only way to escape is to create a success-destiny mind-set day by day, hour by hour."

Today, Darren is living his gift for influencing others into action to achieve their full potential as a sought-after keynote speaker and high-performance business thought leader and coach. He also inspires over 350,000 people around the world through his free DarrenDaily mentoring videos and the thousands of golden nuggets he has collected over the years from the greatest business and personal development leaders, including Richard Branson, Steve Jobs, Elon Musk, Jeff Bezos, Mark Zuckerberg, Howard Schultz, Maria Shriver, and many more.

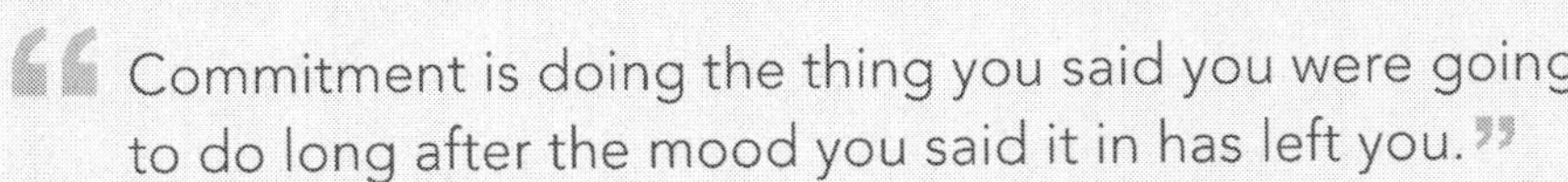

> "Commitment is doing the thing you said you were going to do long after the mood you said it in has left you."
>
> —Darren Hardy

Jigsaw Puzzle

One of the secrets to Darren Hardy's personal and professional success is that he understands the consequence of time—and how to make the best use of time by scheduling priorities for a true work/life balance.

Most of us are pulled in many directions today. Work, school, children's activities, health appointments, grocery shopping—they all are necessary elements of daily life and need to be fit into our schedules. Yet sometimes fitting everything in is akin to putting a jigsaw puzzle together.

Our goal is the image we see once the last piece is in place. Activities are the individual puzzle pieces we use to complete the puzzle one piece at a time. Once we begin grouping similar shades of the pieces together, it's a lot easier and faster to solve the puzzle.

We start by envisioning our ideal week. Most people's ideal week isn't intentionally organized and planned all that thoroughly. A portion of it may be when you need to leave for the office, the time you normally wrap up work, or picking up kids after sports practice. It's all the other stuff in between that chaotically shifts around until we finally find time to take care of it—or not!

When we're not managing our time accomplishing specific tasks throughout our week, the likelihood of getting it all done is slim to none. The fear of committing to a set schedule may feel daunting at first. However, once we realize how much more productive we are, it ends up creating time that wasn't available before. When our to-do list of activities is aligned with our schedule, it's impressive how much we'll get done. However, if we don't take responsibility for how we spend (or waste) our time, we're not likely to get where we say we want to go. More than likely, we'll take care of some things (typically, the easy things), while avoiding the things we consider hard. Hard is usually associated with focus. The good news is we've learned new strategies in Chapter 6 to cultivate more focus. The extraordinary life we want is a result of being in total control of our weekly schedule.

A good way to begin exercising your new scheduling muscles is to start working on your life map. Are you wondering how you'll ever find the time? No problem! You can attack it in one of several ways. I recommend pretending you are working on a looming project deadline and without finishing, you won't be eligible for the quarterly bonus you're banking on. Work first, and then reward. Everything that's not mandatory can be put off for the next few weeks. Of course, you should go to work, unless you have unused vacation time. In that case, you should treat yourself and get away for a few days.

Some things you can give up include TV, reading the newspaper or magazines, social media feeds, your phone (turn it off for blocks of time), socializing (tell your friends you can't see them for a few weeks), housecleaning (cut it to a minimum or hire someone to help), food (eat less-complicated meals or treat yourself to a dinner delivery service), and volunteer commitments (take care of yourself now so you can give your best to others later). You can also get up a little earlier or stay up a little later.

Regardless of how you decide to create your first life map, I have one request:

Please promise yourself you will do it!

It's important to use your time productively. Find a space where you feel good and you are not likely to be interrupted. You may decide to take an entire day away and overnight at a special hotel or resort. Some have gone to local coffee shops, the public library, nice hotel lobbies, or a picnic table at a park on a sunny day. It's well worth the effort. Your family, friends, and co-workers will appreciate the positive changes. You'll love how much better you'll feel when you know the direction you're headed. One of the goals of your life mapping experience should be to find ways to accomplish your goals while keeping your life as simple as possible. Simple means not scheduling unnecessary activities and looking for less-complicated solutions to the responsibilities that are necessary.

Getting Started

We will begin with a blank weekly schedule. The first decision you need to make is the time you will get up each morning and the time you will go to bed each night. Consider the number of hours you need to sleep and still have the energy to reach your goals. It is very difficult to force yourself to perform all your activities, even those you know you want and need to do, when you are tired. Even if you can run on less sleep in the short run, eventually it will catch up to you. You're better off being the tortoise, steady as she goes, rather than doing too much and winding up sick or burned out.

Once you are sure how much sleep is enough, block out those times on the calendar. The *Companion Guide* includes two calendar layouts. One is a portrait layout, the other landscape; work with the format you prefer. You can decide on the time intervals. Some people use fifteen-minute intervals, some thirty-minute, and some one-hour.

Next, add the events that you have no control over. Driving the kids to school at 8:00 A.M. or eating dinner at 7:00 P.M. This is usually where people start underestimating how much time these activities actually take and start feeling claustrophobic. It's necessary to be realistic, so I'm going to suggest you really think through the logistics of each activity. For example, you may eat at 7:00 P.M., but who prepares the meal? If it's you, how long does that take? Be sure to block out time for meal prep. If it's someone else, do you help set or clear the table? Do you clean up and wash the dishes? Completing this schedule is your moment to set reasonable expectations. Continue thinking through each day of the week and weekend and block all the reoccurring activities. Is this making you feel restricted or excited? Hopefully, excited.

Think back to the last time you used GPS directions. You elected to use an app because it helped you decide on a route. That route either helped you get where you were going faster, kept you away from roads or highways you like to avoid, or offered a more scenic trip. It helped you reach your destination. How restricting was that? You followed directions. You decided on a route. You reached your destination. Can you see the parallels between this schedule and that map?

Your schedule is the itinerary you create for your life. When you complete a week on the schedule, you will understand the freedom it brings. You'll be in control of your time. This should bring relief from others trying to *influence* your activities. You'll feel satisfaction as you cross off activities on your list and happiness each day you move closer to achieving your goals.

Priority No. 1: You

Your number one responsibility above all else is yourself! It's critical we take care of ourselves first if we expect to show up with our best for others. I'm only at my best if I'm taking care of myself in all the loving ways I know how. I've learned if I'm not feeling good in my skin, I am not taking care of myself. If I am not taking care of myself, I will not be at my absolute best. The four main areas included in my self-care are workouts, eating healthy, daily practice, and physical beauty. A few of these non-negotiables appear on my Optimal Me list. They may be on your list, too.

My weekly personal training workouts are the No. 1 self-care item on my list. After sleep time is blocked, and my wake time noted, the very next thing written in my weekly schedule is my workout. Three days a week, for forty-five minutes, I work out with my personal trainer, Jason. Jason is a lifeline for me. He is a friend, confidant, listener, advice giver, and great trainer. Even when I'm having a slow-to-get-going morning, Jason knows how to provide me space to just be quiet and grind through my workout.

Maintaining what I call my "natural" weight has not been easy. My parents were both very overweight—obese by clinical standards—and they never exercised. Their diet was unhealthy, our physical genetics aren't ideal, and I had to figure out how to go from obese myself at age nineteen to living a healthy lifestyle and maintaining a healthy weight into my adulthood. I struggled with my weight from age nine to nineteen. A number of factors finally aligned to free me from the wicked weight roller coaster, for one giving up dieting, but it left its mark both physically and emotionally. Those scars never completely go away, but they do slowly fade.

Since I know how much better I feel when my clothes fit comfortably, I carve out time for taking care of my body. That includes blocking time for my workouts, time to shop for and prep food, and time to sit down at the dinner table to enjoy several healthy meals each week with my boys. I'm so much more alive and pleasant to be around when I do this. Likewise, I enjoy treating myself to having my hair and nails done, so I block beauty time in my calendar. Through much trial and error, I've discovered it works best if I carve out a half day, every other week, for personal time. Refocusing after taking a personal break during the workday is a challenge, so I am conscious of how I plan my personal time.

In addition, there are a few other things I know intimately about myself. I'm not a morning person, so I always set client appointments for 11:00 A.M. or after. Late-night hours, from 8:30 to 11:00 P.M., are a productive time for wrapping up my email and computer work for the day. Attending my boys' sporting events is one of my greatest pleasures, so it's a high priority. As soon as the schedule is released, I block their games in my calendar. A huge benefit to being self-employed is having a flexible schedule. It also requires discipline to ensure I work eight or more hours each day. Honoring your priorities, preferences, and personal nuances will serve you in planning your optimal schedule.

It's a Guide

This is a good time to discuss the use of the schedule. It's not meant to be a trap. It's your guide for a more productive and enjoyable journey. It's a way to intentionally work on the activities that support the achievement of your goals. It will help you make the best choices each day.

You should expect to have interruptions to your schedule, even in an ideal week. Depending on your profession, some of you will have interruptions to your schedule daily. If something does come up that takes you off schedule, it doesn't mean the entire day is ruined. Your schedule should help you jump back on track once the distraction is over. Hopefully, you'll feel less confined knowing your schedule is not set in stone. It's meant to be modified to fit your current needs and provide a template for organizing your time.

Daily Planning and Review

The next activity to block in your schedule is something you probably don't have on your Activity List: time for planning and review. Choose the first and/or the last 15 to 30 minutes of each day for reviewing and planning the next. This is how you know if you were keeping pace with your schedule and which activities you completed. Anything left undone can be added to the next day's schedule. This is how we stay on track. Taking time to plan and review is essential to working through our Activity Lists, keeping priorities top of mind, and identifying what's next.

During your review time, you should ask yourself some questions: Were my actions in line with my Principles List? Did I correctly prioritize my activities? Did I complete the things that really matter most? Where can I improve?

Once a week you should invest at least 20 minutes to review the entire week. Weekly check-ins provide an overview of your progress on a scale that is small enough to make any necessary adjustments quickly. Otherwise, if you wait longer, you may veer further off course than you intend.

The time you take to plan and reflect increases confidence, clarifies your activities, offers insight into what's working well versus what needs modification, and reinforces your Goals List—reducing the likelihood of becoming overwhelmed. You'll recognize personal tendencies, your work habits, your ability to focus, and causes for distraction, and find untapped potential where you're excelling. Time set aside for planning and reviewing grounds us for the week ahead and reconnects us to our larger vision.

Block and Manage Time

We can't ignore time management if we plan on improving our efficiency. There are some time management techniques that help us accomplish more in less time. First, everyone has 168 hours each week. How we spend every minute of our day either adds to or pulls us away from what we say is truly important. If we misuse this freedom, we will let ourselves down. We don't get this time back.

How would you feel if you went to your dental appointment at 9:00 A.M. and they told you that the dentist was still in bed? What would you do if they asked you to take a seat in the waiting room and that you would be the third patient he saw when he arrived? What would you think of that dentist? How well did he prioritize his time? Time management is nothing more than setting our priorities straight and completing projects in a timely manner.

Time blocking is synonymous with managing our time, but the key difference is determining blocks of time for working on specific jobs. Ultimately, we need to know what type of structured focus works best. How do you work most efficiently and how does your day typically unfold? Time blocking considers our personal preferences in managing our time. When are you most alert? What tasks require laser focus? Which activities do you enjoy the most or the least?

The following are top tips for time blocking and time management considerations:

- **Preserve your energy.** Don't waste time trying to change things you have no control over. Accept them, adapt to them, and move on.
- **Maintain focus.** Keep in touch with reality. Don't waste time on activities that disconnect you: scrolling social media for hours, watching too much TV, gaming, etc. Occasional down time and distraction is good for you, but chronic use, abuse, or mindless time wasting? That is self-defeating.
- **Guard your emotions.** Repeat activities that increase your self-esteem and avoid those that reduce it. How do you feel about yourself after an activity? If you feel good, you're increasing your self-esteem. You're not looking for how much fun is associated with an activity. What you are looking for is whether the activity has a positive impact on the development of your self-esteem. You are in control; don't blame others or circumstances for activities that lower your self-esteem. Change them!
- **Daily integration.** Use the life mapping tools daily. The forms, Review Card, and *Companion Guide* were created to help you acquire daily habits so that life mapping becomes a natural part of your day. The more frequently you stay on track of your goals, the greater the likelihood you'll accomplish them. Maintain connection to your schedule, life map, and big-picture goals so you remain in control of your day and your life.
- **Plan and review.** Maintain the planning and review habit. Every minute you invest in planning and review will return future time saved. Planning and review continually reinforce your beliefs to enhance your life. Valuing your time and commitment to your schedule works to increase your self-esteem, which benefits you and everyone around you.

- **Minimize interruptions.** Learn to manage unexpected urgent issues. Important interruptions will pop up and, for some, almost daily, but this shouldn't automatically replace activities on your schedule. Attempt to minimize interruptions. Have your calls screened, turn off your cell phone, shut down your email, and return calls, texts, and email during a time reserved for that activity. Learn to leave complete messages and ask that others do the same, minimizing telephone tag. We set the boundaries around our time. If we adhere to those, others will learn to work around our schedule.
- **One master calendar.** A single calendar system is ideal. Many people are completely wireless with their entire schedule and lists are located and accessible on their phone. Some, like me, still carry a planner and utilize electronic scheduling as backup. The ideal time-saver is having one system. However, for the time being, I feel more assured of my schedule having both. I'm so used to seeing everything written down that I appreciate having a planner to take manual notes and see my active lists, as well as receive reminders and alarms about upcoming appointments on my phone. Whatever you use to maintain your schedule should be small enough for you to carry wherever you go. Go with what you know!
- **Optimize your space.** Organize your work area. Everything you use regularly should be within your reach, without leaving your chair.
- **Maximize efficiency.** One of the most dynamic concepts in time management is organizational time. Maintaining an organized business environment and support structures and creating shortcuts will save you many more hours throughout the rest of your month and year. What kinds of shortcuts? For example, compiling an organizational list with activities that are repetitive. Write out instructions for how to complete these tasks systematically. Start identifying the

duties you can delegate. Identify activities that create the biggest savings in time and energy and reduce frustration, and then work on them. Examples include regularly updating your database so your client contacts are always accessible (without searching through email or notes for someone's number), tracking business receipts, paying bills, cleaning up email, or filing.

- **Park your thoughts.** Create a "parking lot" list for all the things you need to do that are not time sensitive. These are things like picking up the clothes from the dry cleaners or scheduling a doctor appointment. You can block time specifically for personal errands, but hiring someone or a service to help save you time is also a great option. Anything that can be ordered online, should be (office supplies, groceries, dry-cleaning pickup and delivery, etc.). Look through your list and see if a service exists to free up your time.

What Is Your Time Worth?

When talking about time, we really need to grasp how valuable it is. Recently, I attended a class where the trainer asked if we knew how much our time was worth. If you're not sure, you'll want to calculate your rate. It's an important number to know to make decisions about the best, most productive, and optimal use of your time and money. Here's how to quickly calculate your hourly value:

Total Annual Income. This should be a net income number if you're self-employed or your after-tax income if you are a W-2 employee, divided by the total number of hours you work per year.

In example one, at $20.00 per hour, this person may consider hiring someone to help with household chores that are easily delegated. If someone else is capable of cleaning for $10–12/hour, it is absolutely worth the return on investment for the additional time it frees up. The higher the hourly value, the greater the ability to hire

TOTAL ANNUAL INCOME			
	Total Net Income	Total Hours Worked	Total Hourly Value
Example 1	$ 40,000	2,000 per year	$ 20.00 per hour
Example 2	$ 75,000	2,000 per year	$ 37.50 per hour
Example 3	$200,000	2,000 per year	$100.00 per hour

skilled help. Start small by passing along the tasks you like the least. Not only will you have additional time for yourself, but you also will have the choice to use the time to work and generate more money or do more of what you love and brings you joy. If you're lucky, they may be one and the same!

Occasionally We Need a Break

Whenever you feel overwhelmed or overscheduled, take a break and look at your week. If you need to adjust the schedule, do it. If, however, it's a temporary event that has caused the discomfort, keep your schedule and adjust that one week. Some people let a hectic week cause them to give up on planning and scheduling. You don't want to make that mistake. Just think about the incredible vision you're working toward and don't let anyone, or anything, remove it from focus.

You will move pieces of the puzzle around many times before you settle in to an ideal weekly schedule. There is no reason to expect to design a perfect schedule the first time around; your schedule will continually change for the rest of your life. Be nimble enough to recognize the need to change and be proactive enough to make the change. Keep stepping back and looking at the whole picture. Ask yourself, "Am I happy with my ideal week?"

CHAPTER TEN

Accountability & Structure

> "I believe that the success of a person is not measured by the amount of money they have nor the things they own. It's measured by the way they live their life to their fullest while loving and lifting others up as they climb."
>
> —John Assaraf

Living Their Gift

Michael had been diagnosed with ADHD as a child. As a young man, he struggled with anxiety and depression. His mental health issues were a carefully guarded secret as he was in the public eye for nearly two decades. However, what he could not keep secret were the controversies that put him on the front pages of national newspapers.

In 2004, he was arrested for driving under the influence and sentenced to eighteen months of probation. In 2009, he was photographed using a bong, the result of which was a lost sponsorship and a three-month suspension from his sport. In 2014, he was again arrested for drunken driving; this time it resulted in a six-month suspension and expulsion from the national team that was readying itself for the World Championships (and eventually failed to qualify).

In early 2018, when he retired from the sport, Michael admitted having contemplated suicide at the height of his career. He recounted how he had sat in his bedroom for five days, not eating and barely sleeping, consumed with one repeating thought: "I don't want to be alive anymore."

Michael Phelps is the most decorated Olympian of all time. He won twenty-eight Olympic medals—twenty-three of them gold—and still holds numerous world records for swimming. Yet his story is a powerful example of the complexity of the mind—how it can both negatively and positively affect our actions and, ultimately, our lives.

Even as Michael struggled with his anxiety and depression, he trained for the tasks at hand, implementing structure and routine to his daily life to be able to compete in—and in his case, dominate—swimming events through four Olympiads. Some actions related to physical activities: eating, warming up his body for races, rehearsing the starting block, and, of course, strengthening his endurance through endless practice in the pool.

Just as important, however, was how he strengthened his mind. Michael often stated that visualization was instrumental in his success. His coach, Bob Bowman, recounted how Michael would mentally rehearse for an upcoming race. "For months before a race, Michael gets into a relaxed state. He mentally rehearses for two hours a day in the pool. He sees himself winning. He smells the air, tastes the water, hears the sounds, sees the clock."

The other key to success was holding on to that vision and supplementing it with positive reinforcement. "When we first started to train together, my coach tried to get me not to say the word 'can't' so I could broaden my mind and believe that I could do whatever I wanted to. I think that was a key of us being so successful."

It was that mental preparation and visualization that propelled Michael into the record books and allowed him to fully live his gift.

> "If you want to be the best, you have to do things that other people are not willing to do."
>
> —Michael Phelps

Act Consistently

Even if you are not a world-class athlete like Michael Phelps, you must have a routine that you stick to religiously and people you can count on to help you maintain structure and discipline. They are key components of the life mapping process, and without them it is much too easy to take shortcuts or diverge on the path to your authentic self.

Accountability and structure provide a baseline like the gas light coming on in your car. It's a friendly reminder of the miles you've driven. It requires you to be diligent by pulling off at the next exit to fill up and squeegee the bugs off your windshield. If you ignore the light, you risk recklessly running on fumes, or worse, you may run out of gas. If you stall out, you'll lose precious time, energy, and money! If that happens, you know the deal . . . your frustration will skyrocket, you'll emotionally beat yourself up because you "knew better," and you'll seriously delay your progress. Some folks may need to experience that chaos a few times before surrendering to the fact that the light is not there to control you but rather to help safeguard the smoothest ride.

If you've gotten this far, you have a sincere desire to live an amazing life. But all the planning, lists, and calendaring in the world won't ensure you're progressing toward your goals. We must perform consistently and progressively. The most ambitious self-starting entrepreneurs, independent contractors, business owners, and executives will admit they benefit from structure and accountability. Researchers' findings say the same thing.

Setting yourself up for success in this area of your life is no different from a professional athlete training with his coach or position-specific trainer, taking an exercise class led by a fitness instructor, or hiring a personal trainer. Most of us push ourselves to higher levels of performance when we have someone we're accountable to who is invested in our excellence.

Our minds and bodies will default to what's easy. Our ancestral survival mechanism naturally reserves energy, so we need prodding to keep moving ourselves forward. Make copies of your life map and put them in strategic locations. Start by placing them where you'll see them daily—on your nightstand, in your daily planner, or on your desk or bulletin board.

Sharing yourself with your friends and family is an important aspect of working toward the goals that matter most. When your life map is complete, consider showing it to supportive people in your life: your boss, family members, and caring friends. Your first instinct will be to keep it a secret. You might think you should wait until you are living it before you tell anyone about it. I encourage you to find at least one person in your life you are comfortable sharing it with, even if it means you are being very courageous in doing so. We all deserve support in the things that matter most.

One of the great benefits of living in alignment with what's most important to us is that people begin to see us differently. Our consistent actions become part of our character and people will recognize our passion and gifts emerging. We'll become known and looked up to for upholding our convictions. In other words, don't be surprised if suddenly people see you as a role model. Once people see us that way, we'll be inclined to continue living that way.

People can't help you if they don't know what you are up to. Opening yourself up involves some risk, but you will find that the people who love you will want to help you. They are on your side. They'll want to see you succeed and be happy. When you show them your life map, it's a perfect time to ask them if they are willing to support you. By asking, you can give specific examples of what you find most helpful in being accountable to living your life map.

You can ask for kindly reminders when your actions conflict with your stated principles or activities. Some people will use words like *realign* or a hand signal such as one finger pointing to the sky or to their eye to mean "I see you and have your best interests at heart." When you hear or see the signal, you immediately know you need to check in with yourself. Did you give that person control over you? No! You gave them permission to help you maintain control over yourself. The final decision will always be yours. You will be very surprised at how willing and encouraging these people will be. You should offer to return the favor if there is any area in which they want support. Remember, you are forming a team to help you create the positive habits that will lead you to your best self.

The stronger you become, the more you will have to share with others. Sharing will speed your development. You will find that the more you give, the more you'll have coming back to you. That is the natural law of reciprocity.

Personal Coaches

You've heard of personal trainers. More than likely, you've also heard of personal coaches. They help people keep their lives in shape by providing structure and accountability. Coaching sessions may occur in person, over the telephone, through the computer (Zoom, Skype, GoToMeeting), or through social media (Facebook Live) on a regular basis. If you have difficulty starting your life map, completing it, or maintaining your schedule, you might consider hiring a personal coach to assist you. A coach can be super beneficial during the habit-forming portion of the process. Once your habits are formed, your need for assistance may diminish, but I believe we always benefit from having a coach.

Personal coaching, also known as business coaching, life coaching, and wellness coaching, along with many other niches developed in the coaching arena, has exploded over the past ten years. I'm a big proponent of personal development from just about any angle. What I like about coaching programs specifically is that they provide reinforcement in areas where we want the biggest boost. You have to be willing to admit where you need help and then find a program that will push you to the next level.

Do your research before you hire anyone. Make sure the person is well respected with positive reviews and testimonials from past clients. Worldwide, there are many types of coaches and varying levels of training and certification. The most widely respected coaching industry training is accredited by the International Coaching Federation (ICF). They hold high standards for ethics as well as specific training requirements and coaching guidelines for member qualification.

However, coaching is an emerging field and there are many excellent coaches and training programs not affiliated with the ICF. A survey conducted in 2015 by PricewaterhouseCoopers LLC reports that about 50 percent of the more than 15,000 survey respondents are members of the ICF. While most people surveyed agree that credentialing is important, approximately 30 percent were not technically certified coaches. The average training the responding coaches received (whether technically certified or not) was 125-plus hours. Regardless, do your homework. If you decide on a coaching program, make sure you understand the type of commitment and cancellation policy before joining.

Peer Accountability

One-on-one accountability partners or small accountability groups also work very well. I've seen many smaller groups emerge through the years in my business as organic spinoffs from attending larger workshops. I mentioned my accountability partners, Cheryl and Brandi. We've been meeting weekly for the past seven years. We attended a larger conference on "Ninja Selling" taught by Larry Kendall in the fall of 2011. A coach trained in Larry's Ninja Selling method started a monthly coaching group in our area.

There were about thirty participants and we were asked to partner up with at least two other people to create an accountability group. That's when Cheryl, Brandi, and I formed our group. Cheryl and I were in the same real estate office but didn't really know each other on a personal level. Brandi was with the same company; however, she worked in a neighboring city with a different ownership and management team, and we didn't know each other at all. None of that mattered, though, since we were merely concerned with surrounding ourselves with like-minded people who cared enough to hold our feet to the fire.

My personal opinion is that a lot of self-employed small-business owners and startup entrepreneurs are not supported in their endeavors. Just because we may be considered self-starters, go-getters, or self-motivated doesn't mean we don't need and thrive on additional support. I think there are millions who would benefit from more accountability and structure. When we are left to our own devices, it's easy to get complacent, and there is a lot to be said for raising the bar. I genuinely believe people will work to achieve higher expectations, especially if they see the benefit. There are a lot of 1099 employees, like me, who love the freedom and flexibility that come with being self-employed. However, I'm 100 percent convinced there's a lot of unmet potential. If you can relate to this, start a small group in your office, reach out to other professionals you admire, and suggest forming your own business accountability group.

Seven years of consistent weekly check-ins has produced three close friends and a deep understanding of where each of us trips up. We are all successful at our jobs, each focusing on unique market niches. We are open books with one another and share best practices, marketing ideas, and insights from recent sales—not to mention sharing tears over personal struggles and curveballs life throws our way. It's invaluable to have their support, both emotionally and professionally.

Another group that spun off of Ninja Selling was within my real estate office. We called it our Ninja Practice Session. A group of ten to fourteen of us met weekly for an hour to practice the selling tools taught at Larry's training. Larry points out that most of us in sales go out into the field and practice our selling skills on our clients. If we are rehearsing in front of our clients, we have not prepared and done our work. We should be showing up confident, polished, and armed with natural responses to client objections!

Our group continued meeting for at least a year and a half. Our Ninja Practice Session prepared us to shine out in the field. As awkward as role-playing can be, our group made it fun and safe, and it was an experimental environment to make mistakes and learn. It's OK to acknowledge that time changes things, and it's unrealistic to expect practice groups or accountability groups to continue forever. We should accept that life and priorities morph over time. If the group's goal is met and people achieve the desired outcome, it's OK to put closure to structured practice. People, places, and things are sure to change, just as our individual journeys will look very different ten years from now. One door closing allows another to open.

What Does Accountability Look Like?

There's an art to being a good accountability partner. Why? There is a big difference between friend and foe when we want and need to be held accountable. A friend will let you off the hook too easily if you didn't do what you said you would do, and a foe will make you feel judged and criticized. The object is to help your partner stay on track, not verbally attack or shame them if they don't. Open-ended questions are always a safe way to help someone gain clarity. It will be much more impactful if each partner is encouraged to seek their own insights into their behavior rather than being told by observation.

I suggest people discuss and decide on the following key points at the beginning of a new accountability partner relationship:

- **How will you meet?** Decide how you will hold your meetings. Will you meet in person? Will you meet over the phone? Will you have a videoconference call?

- **How often will you meet?** Will you check in daily? Weekly? Bimonthly? Monthly?
- **When will you meet?** What time will you hold your accountability meetings?
- **How long will they last?** How long will each meeting last?
- **What will you specifically check in about?** Create an outline of what you'd like to cover during your meetings. Will you be talking about work only? Work and personal life? Fitness goals? Find your primary focus and come to an agreement on what you'll discuss.
- **What format will you use to check in?** For example, in our group we each talk about what transpired over the week both professionally (and whether we accomplished our focus goal) and personally. Once each of us shares, we finish with what our primary focus goal is for the upcoming week.
- **Split the time.** You are striving for efficiency. Your time is limited, so you don't want to be on a runaway call that is about everything but what you're supposed to be talking about. Stay on task and be cognizant of the time. If your call is for thirty minutes, and there are two of you, you should each have 15 minutes to share.
- **Set weekly goals.** Write down what you are committed to accomplishing before your next meeting. What are you planning to do before your next call? If you check in on more than one area, you'll make a weekly focus goal for each area you discuss. It's way too easy to let a few days pass and then completely forget what you said you were committed to. Write it down. Send youself a reminder or a group text or email that lists exactly what priorities everyone's committed to before the next check-in.
- **How do you like to hear feedback?** Initially, share with your accountability partner how you will be most receptive to

hearing feedback if you aren't following through on what you said. This works best if you can give an actual example. It would sound something like this: "Cheryl and Brandi, when I'm not doing what I commit to, it will really help me if you'll say something to me like this: 'Dana, I've noticed for the last two weeks you weren't able to complete the mailing you said you were going to get out. Do you have some thoughts about why it's been OK to let that slide?'" There may be some additional questions you can ask, such as "Is it still something that's important? If so, are you willing to recommit to finishing it this week? Are you willing to check in with us mid-week or would you like one of us to check in with you to see if you've started working on it?" Help your partner by giving them permission to do their job.

- **What motivates you, fear or reward?** Sometimes, when the stakes are high or we've seen disengagement in following through on our commitments, we've set fines. Fear of losing money was more motivating than a prize, so we created a fines worksheet and decided we'd assess one another for incompletions. We established fines for the following: tardiness to the meeting, not notifying or attempting to reschedule more than 24 hours in advance, a total no-show without advance notice, and not completing our weekly goal. Although none of us wanted to give away our money, we made it fun. When we had a task of particular importance, we each had the liberty to increase our own fine. We rotated quarterly who would update the fines worksheet and hold the money. Usually, we donated accumulated fines to charity at Christmastime, and we have also taken ourselves out to lunch as a group.

I'm sure there are a hundred ways to structure and form an accountability meeting. You should be able to come up with a format and time frame that works for everyone. The whole point of spending time to check in is to move yourself and your partner to the next level. If you find that's not happening for one or both of you, you should either self-correct as soon as possible by resetting the ground rules, or politely step out of the group. None of us has the time to participate in activities that don't fill us up and advance our purpose in life. A big part of staying aligned is being proactive and self-correcting when an activity no longer serves us.

Put It into Practice

We can't expect to coast on autopilot on any of the things we've learned in this book simply because we've completed the worksheets and spent some time thinking about our life and goals. Habits are formed by creating a regular practice to bring attention and awareness to everything we declare is important to us, repeatedly.

Here is one last review of the life mapping process you are about to undertake:

1. **Determine your Beliefs List.** The list will grow out of your concept of creation, humanity's purpose, and specifically why you believe you're alive.
2. **Develop your Principles List.** Every principle on the list should be supported by one or more of your beliefs. Without that support, you will be unable to live by your principles when they are tested.
3. **Identify your values.** Core values remind us why we strive to achieve our goals. Choose your top five core values and select one as your leading value. Your Optimal Me and Pure Joy Lists will help bring you back to center when things are out of balance.

4. **Decide on your goals.** List any that come to mind from short term to long term and everything in between. You'll categorize your goals into your major life pillars and prioritize and narrow down your list to extract your primary focus goals.
5. **Discover your magnificent mind.** Select the tools you'll use to strengthen the vision for what you want. Ensure you are mentally prepared to usher in success both consciously and subconsciously.
6. **Create your Activities List.** Crack the boulder! Break down your top priority goals into the manageable activities and tasks necessary to achieve them. Continue to break them into smaller and smaller activities until you can complete each within a week, or preferably a day.
7. **Design an ideal weekly schedule.** Include non-negotiables (sleeping, eating, exercise, family time) and create blocks of time to work on your activities. Update it often and look at it as many times a day as it takes for you to live it.
8. **Create your support system.** Include the people who will help to hold you accountable and encourage your continual forward momentum.
9. **Put it into practice.** Follow the guidelines for developing life mapping habits as a lifestyle by reading, reviewing, and refreshing regularly.

Everything about life mapping is new. Creating new habits is the fastest way to maximize the effectiveness of the process. We are beginners, so it's vitally important we review our life maps over and over and over again. If you're at all familiar with Kumon learning centers, you know that their philosophy is to practice a minimum of fifteen minutes per academic subject *every day*! Yes, every day. That means on your birthday, on the weekend, on religious and nonreligious holidays, and during spring, summer, and winter vacations. That's the difference between ordinary and extraordinary, right? I want *extraordinary* for all of us, but doing the work is up to you!

Life mapping is not about changing who you are every month, quarter, or year. It is about adding depth and creating alignment for the person you are meant to be. Like an artist who adds layers of paint over his original sketch until the image he holds in his mind's eye is achieved, you will continue to add layers of understanding, bringing deeper clarity and meaning to your life. This is a huge opportunity for growth. Your life map is a living document that makes it possible to continually improve without needing to ever start over. As you update your life map, keep your old copies. They become a record of your progress and a historical progression of your legacy.

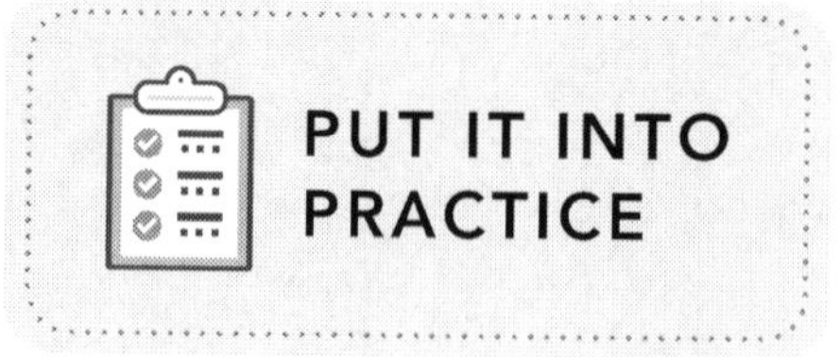

CHAPTER ELEVEN

You Can, and You Will!

> "Do not let what you cannot do interfere with what you can do."
>
> —John Wooden

If you are wondering if you can find meaning, fulfillment, and happiness in this world, you can. If you aren't sure if you're capable of having a happy, healthy life, you are. If you are willing to create your life map and step into your gifts, you'll be an amazing role model and leader for yourself, your children, your friends and family, and the rest of your community.

Life mapping works! It has brought accomplishment, stability, purpose, and a sense of calm to my life and the lives of so many others.

When I pass on to my next life, I won't be compared with anyone, but I will be compared with the person I was capable of being. I will not let myself down and neither should you! Rise up and be the person you were created to be.

How will you know when your map is directing you down the right path? You will know when each day you feel a little calmer and when your daily behavior and actions are ever closer to representing the person you know you are meant to be. And ultimately, when you reflect on your yesterdays without regrets and your tomorrows without fears, then you are on the right path!

Why should we change? Because as long as we have breath, we are not done growing into our full potential! As you change and update your life map, you may want to reread this book. Be patient; there are no quick fixes. As your life improves and things crystallize, your understanding of this material will deepen. You will see and understand things you missed in the first reading. The beneficial, compounding effect of multiple readings will surprise you.

Character Counts

Steve Maraboli, dubbed by *Inc.* magazine as "the most quoted man alive," has a gift with words. His sayings appear in over 3,000 books! Steve's honest and direct style attracts followers from around the globe. He's a best-selling author, consultant, public speaker, and creator of his own method for behavioral change. He's direct and says exactly what's on his mind. I think people are drawn to him because his honesty is refreshing. Making the decision to take the next indicated step (in this case creating your life map after you finish reading the book) is a choice you get to make. Occasionally, we may find those we care about (or ourselves) blaming their unfortunate circumstances on everyone else but themselves. Their "bad luck" is never their fault but always caused by something completely out of their control. This victim mentality is an excuse for not accepting personal responsibility. Steve's quote sums up this mentality well:

> "Today is a new day. Don't let your history interfere with your destiny! Let today be the day you stop being a victim of your circumstances and start taking action towards the life you want. You have the power and the time to shape your life. Break free from the poisonous victim mentality and embrace the truth of your greatness. You were not meant for a mundane or mediocre life!"

In another breath, he says,

> "Your complaints, your drama, your victim mentality, your whining, your blaming, and all of your excuses have NEVER gotten you even a single step closer to your goals or dreams. Let go of your nonsense. Let go of the delusion that you DESERVE better and go EARN it! Today is a new day!"

One Last Story—Mine

My mom was a huge advocate of self-improvement and goal setting. Even though she struggled with depression and prescription drug addiction and never held a job for long, she was a voracious reader and she shared her beliefs with me. Her lessons began when I was a little girl, an impressionable six-year-old.

LESSON ONE: The harder you work, the more money you'll make!

Although my mom's history of employment was spotty at best, the one job she was most proud of was when she was a real estate agent in northern California. It also happened to be the one job she, and everyone who knew her, boasted about because she earned Rookie of the Year at her office in Marin County.

The week before she was scheduled to hold an open house, I would address her invitations. I earned one nickel for every invitation I hand-addressed, stuffed, and sealed. I wrote carefully with my best six-year-old handwriting. Sloppy work wasn't an option. We didn't have a lot of money, so she wouldn't stand for wasting envelopes or doing the same job twice. I thought this was great! If I addressed, stuffed, and sealed 20 letters in an hour, I made ONE DOLLAR!

LESSON TWO: Be your own boss and don't ever depend on a man for your financial security.

When I was ten, I learned how to make picture frames out of fabric. I loved doing crafts. One day, my mom offered to lend me $50 so I could start my own business making "Dana's Frilly Frames." I used the money to purchase supplies: thick matting for the frames, fabric, lace, glue, and batting to puff out the fabric on the front side of the frame. I also designed carbonless custom order forms and had them printed at the local Kinko's.

"Now, Dana," my mom said in her business voice, "you must do the math to calculate how many frames you can make with this material. How much will each cost to make? And what will you need to charge for each frame you sell?" She told me, "This way you can figure out how quickly you will repay this loan and how much money will be left over." I knew it was a big deal for her to offer me $50. Usually, what I heard when I asked for something was, "No, Dana.

We don't have money for that. Our account is already overdrawn by $100."

LESSON THREE: Write down your goals.

My goal was to make and sell twenty frames within two weeks. I eagerly crafted picture frames of various sizes, working whenever I wasn't in school. Once I had a nice selection, I applied Lesson One (The harder I work, the more money I will make). I packed up a tote bag full of frames, my order forms, and a pen. I knocked on door after door until I sold them all. Not only did I come home with enough money to pay my mom back the $50, but I also had money left over to buy more supplies and keep some for myself. I even wrote a handful of pre-sales on my order forms.

LESSON FOUR: Create the vision.

When I was twelve, my mom signed me up for a class at a local church where I learned to create a vision board. The vision board brought my written goals to life. The instructor told us there were a few required elements to a vision board.

1. Acknowledge your spiritual beliefs because there is something greater than yourself that gives beauty to nature, our ability to have life, and an opportunity for us to be and have what we want.
2. Use pictures from magazines or catalogs to capture an image of your goal.
3. Use words to reinforce what you want by choosing words that describe the feeling you will have when you achieve your goal, "as if it's already happened."
4. The clearer and more specific you are, the better.

I would spend hours eagerly flipping through magazines, clipping images to paste on my poster board. I had no reason to question what I was learning because my mom said she'd read lots of books that proved it worked. So that's what I did. I wrote down my goals, made a vision board, and believed that whatever I set my mind to was possible to achieve.

Many of my accomplishments I attribute to being driven and having a goal-setting mindset. But my innate desire for achievement was often distracted by instability in our home. My dad was hardly around after I turned nine and never around after I turned twelve. He couldn't find a job in Seattle after we'd already moved from southern California. He boomeranged to his old job so they'd have money to pay rent, and he only flew up every few months to spend the weekend with us.

I was the youngest of five kids and by the time I was twelve, the last of my older siblings, Cara, moved away from home. It was the summer before I was set to start junior high when all hell broke loose. One of the weekends my dad was home visiting, Cara confided in my older sister Lisa (who is twelve years older than me) that my dad had been molesting her since she was thirteen. (My brothers and sisters had different dads, so Cara wasn't his biological daughter.) Lisa promptly told my mom, and before I knew what happened, my dad was on the next flight to LA, never to return.

Even with weekly counseling, the effects of lingering childhood trauma riddled my tween and teenage years. My motivation was hot and cold, on and off, good one day and bad the next. After a few years living alone with my mom, and her mental illness worsening, my own mind was drowning in suicidal thoughts. My mom's deepening depression, prescription drug addiction, constant money problems, inability to keep a job, hypochondria, and the sad, dark home I'd walk into after school offered me little else than a terrifying feeling of hopelessness. Most days, my mom wasn't out of bed before four in the afternoon.

Several months before my sixteenth birthday, my counselor initiated a family meeting of sorts. My brothers and sisters and mom were there, and everyone agreed with his assessment that my mom was not providing a stable home. I was told I should find somewhere else to live or I'd likely end up in a foster home. I was frantically dialing friends and family to find somewhere to go. I was scared but also relieved to be out from under the deathly cloud that hung over my mom's home.

Fortunately, and I do give my mom a lot of credit for this, I clung onto a handful of her positive beliefs that helped guide me. Even through years of emotional roller-coaster rides, and bouncing around in search of stability, I experienced a handful of victories in junior high and high school. Some of these wins included participating in student government; cheerleading; and being selected to attend weeklong trips on scholarship to New York City for a DECA marketing conference, the Wharton School of Business in Pennsylvania for an entrepreneurship camp, Fort Warden, Washington, for a summer writing program, and Salt Lake City, Utah, to compete in the national DECA competition in business plan writing. I wish my mom would have had the strength to hang on to her beliefs, too, but sadly she died by suicide just a few days before I graduated from high school.

Finally, after many years of feeling like I was hugging the shoulder of a very jagged cliffside road, I made a decision that blessed me with stability and a renewed sense of self-confidence. I was nineteen, extremely overweight, and floundering in college because I felt smothered in debt. Intuitively, I knew unburying myself from my debt coffin would bring relief. So I answered an ad in the college paper about a seafood processing job in Alaska.

They hired me on the spot after I passed a physical and a drug test. The next thing I knew my duffle bag was packed with some clothes, a

Walkman, a little makeup, a brand-new pair of brown rubber Grundens rain boots, and a set of bright-orange rain gear. After two commercial airplane rides, a choppy water landing in a seaplane, and a bumpy ride in an aluminum skiff, I climbed up the metal ladder attached to the hull of the *M/V Tempest*, which was anchored in a remote Aleutian Island called Akutan.

Opening the door to my four-person bunkroom was as if I found home for the first time in my life. Boat life was easy, and I felt pampered in comparison to life on my own. All our meals were prepared by galley cooks, our clothes were washed and folded, my stateroom was up two flights of stairs from where I worked on the production line, I didn't need a car, and there wasn't anywhere to spend money except for a few dollars in the ship's store that was open twice a week for candy and snacks. The heavy weight of my childhood began melting away, and I reconnected with my passion for accomplishment.

I spent enough time at sea over five years to become licensed by the U.S. Coast Guard as chief purser. I moved up the ranks from a crab processor aboard a thirty-five-person crew to chief purser (a fancy way of saying office manager) of the largest floating Alaskan processor at the time with 225 crew members. I met my first husband, Patrick Corbett, when I was twenty, studied for and passed the Washington real estate exam when I was twenty-three, and accumulated enough credits during the fall months (when the boat was in drydock in Seattle/Tacoma) to earn my associate degree at twenty-five.

Ready to start a family and settle into a more normal land-based life, I left Alaska for the last time to start my full-time real estate career. Pat and I set out to get pregnant right away and he switched seafood companies for a job based in Seattle with a lot less travel.

My goal-setting mind-set was alive and well throughout my twenties, but as I approached thirty I became unsettled. As my career started taking off, I felt myself pulling away from Pat. My personal desire to constantly push myself to do and be more, and want the same for those around me, drove me away from Pat's contentment with consistency and simplicity. Not seeing how we could co-exist with our polar-opposite preferences, I decided to leave the marriage after we'd been together for nine years. Even so, I still loved and respected Pat.

I also clearly recognized a distinction between my job as a career that pays the bills, and my purpose in life, which renders meaningful fulfillment and joy. I was newly single; a full-time working mother with a two-year-old son; and a co-parent with my former husband. Unsure of where my future was headed, I felt unsettled at my core. That's when I drove to the bookstore in search of enlightenment and direction, and I discovered *Life Mapping*. The book was so compelling that I immediately created the first version of my life map without hesitation and have updated it yearly ever since. It was the millennial year, symbolic of a fresh start, and it launched me forward exponentially.

Over the years, I've continued to engage in leadership workshops, counseling, and personal coaching, and I've embraced several other helpful insights and practices along the way. Some are more introspective like yoga and mindfulness, and others are more action-oriented like journaling and teaching. Now, after nearly two decades of relying on my life map for direction, it's evolved into a very meaningful personal document. Looking back now, I see I've captured footsteps of my life's journey.

Over the last thirty years I've made a ritual of taking a day to an entire weekend (usually in December) to plan for the year ahead. About six years ago, in 2012, I invited agents from my real estate office to join me for a half-day of business planning. I bought everyone a copy of *Life Mapping* and encouraged them to read it. We used the book as our reference point—the "bible," if you will—for the optimal technique in structuring goals.

It's interesting to note that I am a deep introvert by nature. My demeanor at the office is typically head down with an aura of "Do not disturb me; I'm working." I've come to learn through sharing my passion that people now see me in a very different light. I was never too busy to share how goal setting was the primary catalyst of my professional success and other meaningful accomplishments throughout my life. As a matter of fact, once I stepped into "planning" mode for our retreats, I entered "the zone." It's a zone where my creativity flows. Half-day meetings soon transitioned into full-day meetings, and now they are full-blown two-day destination retreats. My internal light shines when I'm leading workshops. Like Bill says, I'm living more in alignment with who I was created to be. My glow is a direct result of believing I'm making a meaningful impact on others' lives as I share my passion.

In 2015, I approached my designated broker to ask what he thought about moving our business planning to a local resort. I love beautiful settings, especially those surrounded by water, and Alderbrook Resort in Hood Canal, Washington, is an idyllic retreat. I had already planned to get away for two days, so I thought, why not open it up to others?

In 2015, I declared at my company's first overnight business planning retreat that I thought it would be a good idea to reach out to the author of *Life Mapping*, Bill Cohen, to see if I could get "certified" in his method, if such a thing existed. The first time the idea appears on one of my life maps is in 2013. I stunned myself by saying this out loud and then felt ashamed when I didn't act on it for almost two years. I think I imagined being certified would somehow bring more credibility to what I was sharing. The truth was I'd experienced many intuitive nudges that speaking and writing needed to be part of my life's journey. Even though I accepted the notion as truth, I didn't possess the courage or tools to work through my doubts and insecurities.

I carried feelings of shame for nearly two years for not acting on what I announced in 2015. It helped me realize something very important. This below-the-surface disappointment in myself developed because my inaction violated several fundamental principles of mine: I will do what I say, I will only make commitments I can keep, and I will do things I am fearful of as a practice of showing up "big" in the world. My guilt was a soulful reaction to being out of alignment. This is exactly why Bill Cohen wrote *Life Mapping*!

Now, I'm not suggesting that carrying around icky feelings of shame for two years is a good idea. However, what I learned is my internal compass is spot on WHEN I LISTEN TO IT. The problem was, I didn't quite understand why I wasn't acting on it. Over those two years, my wise internal voice became louder and louder, saying things like, "Dana, you need to write and share your story. You need to do something with your childhood journals you've been carrying around for thirty years." But I still defiantly chose to ignore it.

I firmly believe inaction and self-sabotage occur when we carry limiting beliefs and don't step forward into our fear. These limiting beliefs are often subconscious, and they will stifle, slow, and paralyze progress even when we say we want change. In the case of not reaching out to Bill Cohen, I had held onto an old belief that if I can't safely be assured of some level of success, I shouldn't even try. I've played "small" in my life in many areas (up until recently) because of my limiting beliefs (part of a fixed mind-set) and negative self-talk. This nasty little devil of a doubter would say things to me like "What if you don't get it right? What if you fall flat on your face and look stupid? What if people don't like you? What do you have to say that people will want to hear?"

The reality is, I still get stuck and struggle with some of life's challenges. Let's be real, A LOT of life's challenges. Therefore, I'm not perfect. Reality check, Dana: We are all perfectly imperfect! It's not an easy concept to grasp for an adult healing from gaping wounds resulting from childhood trauma; however, I am learning to accept my shortcomings as I lovingly and wholeheartedly do for others. Fortunately, another belief I hold dear is that my life is for continually learning. Gaining awareness of my limiting beliefs, acknowledging they no longer serve me, and practicing new, scientifically supported methods to rewire my thinking is allowing me to step into my fear.

Moving toward my wise voice means now I am living . . . not simply existing! *Live Your Gift* is in print because I surrendered to my fear and willingly took the necessary actions. I stepped into faith. It's an indescribable feeling I want to share with others who may also be stuck. My heart is full, knowing I am now, finally, living in alignment with my beliefs and putting my gifts to work.

I'll end my personal story—my "Living Their Gift"—just as I have ended the other stories throughout this book. It's what I have come to believe about the universe and why I am where I am today.

> "The day you were born, there was a reason planted deep inside your soul. Let it grow with nurturing and self-love, and it will blossom from the light of discovering who you are destined to become."
>
> —Dana V. Adams

CHAPTER TWELVE

The Authentic You

> "The authentic self is the soul made visible."
>
> —Sarah Ban Breathnach

You are an amazing spirit! No one else has your unique gifts. Understanding who you are, who you can be, and how you fit into the world requires you to step back and look at the bigger picture.

Remember:

Our **beliefs** are the core of who we are as human beings. They represent what we consider to be our universal truths and the reason we're alive. Beliefs are the reasons we follow our principles.

Our **principles** are our rules for life, our personal playbook, our inner GPS, and the behaviors we have chosen to live by and want to follow. Principles are the signposts that we will use to make decisions when we come to forks in the road.

Our **values** are those standards and behaviors we deem as important in life. Values are the things that make our lives more enjoyable and the reasons we have the goals we do. When our values align with our actions, our authentic life shines through.

Our **goals** are what we're striving to achieve, learn, or acquire to support our core values. The underlying theme behind goal setting is to take control and then maintain control of our life. Beliefs, principles, and values are the foundation upon which we build our goals. They are achieved not only through our focused efforts but also with universal support.

Our **magnificent mind** is used to strengthen the vision for what we want. It helps us identify limiting beliefs, in order to subdue self-defeating thoughts that sabatoge our best intentions. It also helps us reframe our brain's thought patterns.

Life mapping is the way to an authentic life. It helps us identify where our goals and actions may be out of alignment with our fundamental beliefs, principles, and values. To be successful in the life mapping process, you must continually put in the work.

Remember:

The **activities** we do every day define us, our character, and our contribution to the world. Goals are like boulders, and activities are the chunks of rock that break off when the Earth moves. Activities without goals are like aimless darts, and goals without activities are dreams; when activities and goals are interconnected, everything is possible!

A **schedule** is your guide for a more productive and enjoyable journey. It's not meant to be a trap. It's a way to intentionally work on the activities that support the achievement of your goals. It will help you make the best choices each day.

We must have **accountability and structure** in our lives. We must have a routine that we stick to religiously and people we can count on to help us maintain structure and discipline. Accountability and structure provide a baseline for achieving our goals, and without them it is much too easy to take shortcuts or diverge from the path to our authentic self.

And finally, our **gifts** are what make us unique. They are those special skills we have that allow us to do some things better than most other people. At times, they may be locked away, just waiting for the chance to shine, but all of us absolutely, positively have gifts. Are you ready to live yours?

> "For what it's worth: It's never too late to be whoever you want to be. I hope you live a life you're proud of, and if you find that you're not, I hope you have the strength to start over."
>
> —F. Scott Fitzgerald

DANA'S LIFE MAP • PAGE 1 OF 2

BELIEFS

- I believe everything happens for a reason
- I believe nature is a reflection of God and God's power
- I believe there is a God-given purpose for my life
- I believe in karma—what goes around comes around
- I believe my life is for continual learning
- I believe my life is interconnected with others' lives and the impact stretches well beyond
- I believe my life is for working through issues I have not yet mastered in previous lives
- I believe everyone wants to be loved, appreciated, and acknowledged
- I believe in evolution in nature and in people's souls
- I believe I have an ability to make a positive impact on other people's lives
- I believe people deserve a second chance and have the ability to change their lives
- I believe I am the mother of my children by God's divine plan and they have chosen me as their mother
- I am in control of my thoughts and actions and I am not in control of nature and other people
- I believe I choose my destiny in life
- I believe God speaks to me to guide my choices in life - it is my choice to listen
- I believe living in alignment with our soul produces a heightened sense of joy
- I believe everyone has a gift to contribute to the world

PRINCIPLES

- I only make commitments I can keep
- I learn from my mistakes
- I put family first and I make an effort to be present with them
- I share my story with others
- I am authentic and live my life with the utmost integrity
- I challenge myself by always having willingness to learn
- I support my children for their unique gifts in the world
- I am an example for my kids of a hard work ethic and appreciating the things I have
- I am loving toward my children and partner and show them physical and emotional affection
- I listen to and honor my inner voice
- I find peace and satisfaction in organization, structure and balance
- I am financially blessed as a result of my hard work
- I love and let others love me
- I make amends as quickly as possible
- I set boundaries that honor my values
- I value balance of my time between family, work, and personal care
- I connect with God every day and pray to be guided by His will for me, and I share spirituality with the boys
- I am intentional with my kids about listening to what they have to say
- I spend time and energy on things within my control
- I respect my natural environment and acknowledge its beauty when I observe it
- I treat others how I want to be treated—talked to, cared for—loved and I connect intentionally
- I see the greatness in people and acknowledge their contributions
- I consciously work to moderate my reactions during upset to stay present
- I keep my body at its optimal health and wellness by staying fit and eating clean 85%+ of the time
- I practice spirituality daily
- I do things I am fearful of as a practice of showing up 'big' in the world

PURE JOY!

- **Babies:** Holding, loving, being in tune with their needs, hearing them on a soul level
- **Water:** Sight, how it looks, moves, reflects, sounds (lapping, crashing, splashing)
- **Landscaping:** Manicured landscapes, pesentation of beauty, colors, heights, shapes, different types merged together, yet still separate
- **Baking:** Smells of sweets, baking, creation of something from nothing, changing form, taste, giving, tradition, nurturing to me
- **Music:** Love to listen to music, marks time in my life, picks me up, elevated mood
- **Kids' Activities:** Love to be there in support, love to love them w/o expectation of outcome
- **Yoga:** How I feel afterward, breathing to regulate body/mind, community, spiritual time, physical workout, mental challenge, spiritual and emotional release
- **Walks:** How I feel afterward, taking in nature, walking by the water is best!
- **Crafting:** Cards, baked goods, sewing, giving
- **New Homes:** Environment, feel, smell, touch, textures, creation, formation, vision design, building something from nothing, frames people's lives
- **Sunsets & Beautiful Clouds:** Appreciate amazing colors and incredible designs and shapes

OPTIMAL ME

- Make my bed
- Work out 3-4x a week and weights 2x a week+
- Car clean 1x every 7-10 days
- Checkbook up to date within 10 days
- Intentional time with kids, kiss goodnight, affection, listening
- Dinner with the family 3-4x a week
- Reading to learn
- Church/yoga
- Writing gratitudes daily
- House picked up
- Returning emails within 24 hours

CORE VALUES

2018	2017	2016
Financial Security	Family	Personal Development
Emotional Well-Being	Financial Security	Accomplishment
Family	Integrity/Authenticity	Genuine
Integrity	Balance/Freedom/Flexibility	Grace/Calm
Freedom/Balance	Organization	Spirituality

Life Mapping Workbook — live your gift

DANA'S GOALS • PAGE 2 OF 2 *BOLD DENOTES 90-DAY FOCUS GOAL

FAMILY

- Golfing with boys, lessons and range
- Boston
- Build a new home or remodel in downtown Kirkland
- Weekend getaways: Alderbrook & Seabrook
- Build a waterfront home on Lake Ave.
- Touch base w/kids regarding homework and grades
- Family picture w/professional photographer in Hawaii
- Travel to a country outside the US with the kids
- Provide opportunity for Younglife camp
- Eat together as a family at least 3-4 times a week
- Kids helping with 100 mailings per week
- Symphony, ballet, theater four times a year
- Have friends and family over to the house monthly
- Review spirituality intent/church or other?
- Vision boards with kids
- **College for all kids or supporting them in their passions • tours**
- Great Wheel & Seattle Waterfront
- Tulips
- Cook w/boys—teach them how to cook
- Karate boards for boys
- Print all photos in photo boxes for each son
- Bellevue Candy Shop Parlor
- Volunteer with boys
- Painting with boys 1-2x per year
- Goals list for boys & family
- Secured housing plan
- Schedule Hawaii trip
- Holiday show with the boys
- Seahawks game
- Pike Street
- Le May Car Museum
- Seattle Chihuly Glass Museum
- Summer jet skiing
- Paddle arboretum
- UW football game with all
- WSU football game at Pullman
- Maeto November event w/boys
- Fishing, regular or fly w/boys
- Tune piano
- Finish going through kids' garage papers
- White sporty shoes
- Bedspreads for the boys

CAREER

- Reach earning goal
- Land to Luxury Facebook page live
- Five Star Logo on email signature with Land to Luxury
- Marketing plan specifically for Kirkland NC Facebook page
- Send 400 mailings or emails of value every month
- Average sales price of $1.2M or higher
- Time-block my weekly calendar
- New-construction listing agent niche
- Website update
- Write Companion Guide
- **Write book: *Live Your Gift***
- Builders linked on Windermere or Facebook page
- Branding collateral: letterhead, envelopes, note cards
- Catalog all past writing
- Builder & Luxury Client presentation folder
- Marketing calendar systems in place
- Writer's workshop
- Builder credentials
- Kids photo on website
- List a $5M property
- Accountability group to continue weekly
- Coaching with Jessica
- IRS quarterly payments on time
- Alderbrook Group quarterly follow up throughout the year
- Auto-emails monthly
- Sell a lot for a $5M new construction listing in Kirkland
- Next Life Map complete by December 31
- Sphere updated
- Five Star Profile complete
- Update testimonials through 2018
- Create buyer/seller testimonial sheet
- On-site photos for new construction
- Ice cream-yogurt shop during retirement

LIFE MAPPING

- Life Mapping Institute
- Life Mapping Institute Facebook page
- One writing weekend per month through March
- Competitive Landscape complete
- Book publishing commitment
- Book proposal written by April 30
- Phase II goals complete by April 30

SPIRITUAL

- Personal growth videos/podcasts weekly
- Take walks along the lake 1x week
- Flowers at house, fresh, twice a month or more
- Cooking classes
- Read books that expand my knowledge-12+ per year
- Two charity auctions
- Counseling monthly
- Paint dress for Megan
- Embellish paintings
- Self-acceptance work on body & co-dependence
- Writing my book
- Writer's workshop
- Read relationship book/workbook
- 12-Step meetings—Co-Dependence and Alanon
- Peace with my past
- Public speaking
- Daily practice of Evening Visualization
- Daily gratitudes & idea book in bathroom
- Read daily meditation
- Journaling

PHYSICAL

- Body fat to 17% or under
- Work out: cardio 2x week (walk, yoga, stairs, etc.)
- Train with weights 3x week
- Brows, 6x year
- Nails every two weeks
- Pedicures every two weeks
- Hair every six weeks

SECURITY/FINANCIAL

- Net worth goal
- Live within my means
- **Pay quarterly taxes • save each sale**
- College funds for the boys full
- Contribute to retirement on every sale
- Credit score + 20pts
- Update car

MATERIAL WANTS

- Small & medium serving bowls
- White purse
- Jewelry: earrings, bracelets, necklaces
- Work skirts 4
- White business tops
- Flower pots always planted
- Black boots, thicker heel, rounder toe
- New belts
- Peep-toe pumps
- Family room couch
- Lulu pants (2)
- Patent pumps
- Recover dining room chairs & re-sturdy
- Pearl bracelet
- Long brown work winter coat
- Kids clothes shopping
- New spring trench coat
- Neutral-color pumps
- Going-out jackets—2
- 2 new yoga tops
- King-size duvet
- Halter swimsuit
- Bucket hat for Trent-10 Diamond Lax
- Clarisonic
- Briefcase for work
- Speakers working outside
- Purple Adams jersey w/bling
- Lace tanks black and white
- Glasses
- Rhinestone for pink watch
- Hiking shoes
- Dining room rug
- Rocking chair
- Business pants—3 pair

Life Mapping Workbook  live your gift

Acknowledgments

To my wonderful Windermere Real Estate Kirkland friends who came together to inspire *Live Your Gift*. Thank you for offering me a platform to express and share my passion for life mapping. Your willingness to join me on this odyssey of self-discovery is one of the primary reasons I was able to write this book.

Laura Brodniak, the timing and generosity of your offer to attend Jessica Butts's Front Seat Life Event was divine intervention. Rays of sunshine beamed right through the sheets of rain that day, providing an undeniable sign it was time to honor my intuition.

Jessica Butts, I'm inspired by your spunky confidence. You give me hope and courage watching you be "unapologetically who you are." Thank you for gathering an incredible group of supportive women around us. Your structure and coaching came at such an opportune time.

Karen Lynn Maher, we'll both remember the day we first met at your book circle. My tears were falling, but you held a safe space that cradled my awakening. Thank you for standing beside me while I became steady on my own two feet. Your swift guidance allowed me to plant many seeds. Flowers are popping up everywhere and blooming a rainbow of brilliant colors.

Milena Hrebacka, you were a patient saint working telepathically to absorb my mental images. I appreciate your hanging in there to produce the book cover, companion guide, and worksheet designs I love.

Nikki Closser, your talent behind the lens, and Lisa Fischer, your eye for style, perfectly captured the essence of my future self.

Jeni Dahn, I love you for helping me set my little girl free.

Bill and Gail Cohen, your welcome reception to my bold request was a blessing beyond anything I could have imagined. "Thank you" will never convey the bundled-up excitement I feel inside. It's like I'm a little girl peeking around the corner on Christmas morning to see a beautifully lit tree, lots of presents spilling out from underneath the branches, and stockings overflowing with surprises. I'm certain the mystery of what lies ahead will be filled with the same childlike delight as unwrapping presents. Your blind faith in our crossing paths allowed me to trust that this was meant to be.

Darren Hardy, thank you for welcoming me and training me at HPF 23. I have immense gratitude and respect for how you care about the success of others. Your introduction to Reed Bilbray was like asking me to make a wish and then granting it. Julie Ward-Glenn, you're truly a VIP maven and a fairy godmother.

Reed Bilbray, my publisher, what an absolute pleasure working with you. Thank you for your professionalism, steady confidence, and leadership. Your expertise allowed me to relax throughout the process knowing you were at the helm. You assembled a fabulous team. Not only did they support me, but I felt carried to the finish line.

Judy Emmert, my editor extraordinaire, your gift transformed my canvas of pastel colors into a beautiful seaside landscape. You instinctively detected my whisper and gracefully invited my voice to come alive and capture the essence of living our gifts.

Kim Baker, thank you for your graphic wizardry in formatting the book and companion guide layout and contributing the finishing touches on all design elements. Your ability to extract the images dancing in my mind and render them visible and transformed on paper is a gift I truly admire and appreciate

Katherine Vincent, Cheryl Nygaard, Brandi Chambers, and Mike Connolly, thank you for your unwavering friendship and for believing in me.

To my kindred souls from the valley of the Enchantments, thank you for allowing me to know what it feels like to be home.

Eric Mellin and Lisa Mach, I'm a very lucky little sister. Your love is nurturing, constant, and protective like a one-hundred-sixteen-year-old oak tree.

James, Trent, Gage, and Michael, thank you for supporting me in this endeavor. You encouraged me by never voicing any doubts and patiently listened to my ramblings about all I learned in the process. May we all experience living our gifts!

Thank you all so much! I am eternally grateful.

Recommended Reading

Life Mapping by Bill Cohen

The Answer by John Assaraf & Murray Smith

The Language of Letting Go by Melody Beattie

Daring Greatly by Brené Brown, PhD, LMSW

Live Your Life from the Front Seat by Jessica Butts

Parenting with Love and Logic by Foster Cline & Jim Fay

The Miracle Morning by Hal Elrod

The Compound Effect by Darren Hardy

Darren Hardy's *Insane Productivity* Course + *High Performance Forum*

Platform by Michael Hyatt

Facing Codependence by Pia Mellody

The Slight Edge by Jeff Olson

Tinker Dabble Doodle Try by Srini Pillay, M.D.

The 5 Second Rule by Mel Robbins

The Four Agreements by Don Miguel Ruiz

Diets Don't Work by Bob Schwartz

About the Author

Dana V. Adams is the founder of the Life Mapping Institute and considered one of the country's top thought leaders on the life mapping process. For decades, first as a student and now as a teacher and mentor, Dana has inspired, empowered, and led thousands to embrace their life's gifts to live happy, abundant, and authentic lives.

After becoming a licensed real estate agent in 1993, Dana discovered the life mapping process reading Bill Cohen's book, *Life Mapping*. Combining the power of the life mapping process with her caring attitude, responsiveness, professionalism, stellar customer service, and dogged determination, Dana built an award-winning real estate business. She excels in the specialty niche of "Land to Luxury," selling in-fill land and development property, and marketing the new homes once built. Dana has distinguished herself as a six-time recipient of the Five Star Real Estate Agent Award, Managing Broker, Master Certified New Construction Specialist, Luxury Marketing Specialist, and Master Certified Negotiation Expert, and is a member of the National Association of Realtors.

A native of Southern California, Dana grew up around commercial fishing. She moved to Kirkland, Washington, with her family in 1979, and after high school worked in the Alaskan fishing industry. She is a graduate of the University of Washington with a degree in business management and marketing. Still living in her hometown of Kirkland, Dana loves taking long walks along the shores of Lake Washington and living a healthy, active lifestyle.

Aside from her four sons, Dana's passions are a lifelong pursuit of personal development and community service. She has organized community-wide events on opiate awareness and served on the City of Kirkland Task Force Boards for sidewalks and affordable housing. She currently sits on the EvergreenHealth Youth Mental Health Task Force and has written for *Kirkland Living* magazine.

www.danavadams.com

Share *live your gift*

Give to Family and Friends

Almost all of us have better odds of completing new endeavors with a little support and guidance. Consider giving *Live Your Gift* to a friend, a family member, or your partner and make your life maps together.

Plan a Business Event

If you are a business owner or manager, consider giving *Live Your Gift* to your team. I'd love to facilitate your on-site or off-site life mapping event.

Register for a Workshop

Some of us need more encouragement, structure, and even a little hand-holding. That's me for sure and I'm not ashamed to say it! If you're like me and absorb material more comprehensively by attending a class, you can visit my website and register for a live workshop. The workshops are experiential because you will create your life map and motivational because participants benefit from the collective energy and interaction of the group. It's a powerful sharing and personal growth experience in the company of like-minded people who want to live life—*on their terms.*

ALSO:

Live Your Gift Companion Guide

Remember, the *Live Your Gift Companion Guide* helps you complete all the activities outlined in the book. The beautifully designed workbook is full of guidance, inspiration, and all of the necessary worksheets. If you're a self-starter and have success working independently, consider purchasing the *Live Your Gift Companion Guide*. You've come this far, so reward yourself by creating your personal life map. You can either buy the color print edition or download a PDF version.

If you've enjoyed this book, please consider leaving a review on Amazon. Even if it's only a few sentences, your time and willingness to share your thoughts will help ensure others learn about *Live Your Gift*, too.

For more information, please visit www.lifemappinginstitute.com.

LIFE MAPPING
INSTITUTE

37457934R00135

Made in the USA
San Bernardino, CA
30 May 2019